THE
WORLD'S BEST
INSPIRING
STORIES

G. FRANCIS XAVIER

W0007227

JAICO PUBLISHING HOUSE

Ahmedabad Bangalore Chennai
Delhi Hyderabad Kolkata Mumbai

Published by Jaico Publishing House
A-2 Jash Chambers, 7-A Sir Phirozshah Mehta Road
Fort, Mumbai - 400 001
jaicopub@jaicobooks.com
www.jaicobooks.com

THE WORLD'S BEST INSPIRING STORIES
ISBN 978-81-7992-921-6

First Jaico Impression: 2009
18th Jaico Impression (New Cover): 2021
19th Jaico Impression: 2022

Printed by
Trinity Academy For Corporate Training Limited, Mumbai

Dedicated to
Mr. Anand Sanjay Malik and his Family
with
Love and Affection

CONTENTS

CONTENTS

CONTENTS

FOREWORD

I was one of the many who attended the introductory session of "Tap Your Genius"—a personality development programme. My wife and I were tremendously impressed by the demonstration.

We enrolled for the programme immediately. The programme, conducted by Dr. G. Francis Xavier, covered several key areas including time and stress management, memory and brain power, health and happiness.

The lecture demonstration was interspersed with many anecdotes to inspire and motivate the participants.

Dr. Xavier is an adept at narrating stories and has quite a few appropriate ones for every occasion.

When I asked him one day, "Doctor, how many stories do you know?" He said "Must be more than ten thousand."

This book you are holding is the result of Dr. Xavier's persistent efforts at reading literally thousands of books and attending innumerable seminars, workshops and programmes around the world.

Some of the stories from Dr. Xavier's treasury have been included in this book on the insistence of many Tapponians (beneficiaries of Dr. Xavier's course Tap Your

Genius) including myself.

This book contains fantastic collection of stories from around the world drawn from all strata of human society. The stories come in handy and, in my opinion, they can be narrated to entertain guests at parties, while making business presentations, when writing a personal letter or telling children something of interest.

I have read and re-read every story while preparing them for the press. Let me reiterate-you are holding a gold mine. The gold remaining in the gold mine is of no use unless you mine and use the metal.

With wishes for success and happiness.

P. P. Hebbar
Chairman
ASPA Group of Companies

PREFACE

I conduct a training programme called TAP YOUR GENIUS. This is a multi-dimensional Personality Development Programme designed to ignite the spark of genius in the participants. A variety of techniques, drawn from the Eastern wisdom of yogic lore and the Western system of scientific research, is offered to the participants. One of the effective techniques is STORY MEDITATION. Stories pregnant with the philosophy and practices of self-improvement will be presented. The end part of the story is not given immediately and the participants are asked to come out with their answers. They are made to ponder and relate to their own life situations. This technique is found to be very effective in changing the thought-patterns and thereby inducing an irresistible desire for betterment.

I have followed the same procedure here. The reader is urged to go through each story with an open mind, guess possible answers to the questions given at the end of each story and verify with the answers given. It is important to ponder over the message of the story rather than skim through the pages for mere entertainment.

A Note to Parents: Offer this book to your children as a precious gift. They would love to read these stories.

In the process, they would also improve their personality considerably without your 'sermon'.

Dr. G. Francis Xavier Ph. D.

358, 8th Main, Viveknagar
Bangalore-560047
Mob. 09449544358/09343721820
E-Mail-gfrancisxavier@yahoo.co.in

ACKNOWLEDGEMENT

I owe a deep sense of gratitude to all those who have been a source of inspiration and encouragement in my literary pursuit.

I sincerely thank Mr. P. P. Hebbar for writing an appropriate foreword for this book.

I am extremely thankful to the Publisher, Mr. Akash Shah and, the Chief Editor of Jaico Publishing House, Mumbai, Mr. R. H. Sharma, for bringing out this book in an excellent manner.

In addition, I wish to express my deep sense of gratitude to all my friends and the participants of my various training programmes. They are too large in numbers for me to list all the names individually. However, the following persons deserve special mention. The names are given in an alphabetical order for easy reference.

Acharya V, Amudha P. Kandasamy, Arpudamary, A. Arulmarianathan, Babu K., Verghese, Bharat Kapasi, Bishop Joseph D'Silva (late), Bro. Jacob Ezhanikat, R. Devaraj, Elgy Danny, Emmanual Das, Ethirajulu Naidu, Gangaram Naik, P. Gasper, K. J. George, Fr. Giri Raju, Gnanedrakumar, Gunakodi Sekar, Ilyas Montri, Dr. Jagannath Rao, Jaiprakash Tiwari, Fr. Jayanathan, John

Joseph, Dr. M Joseph, I Joseph Victor, K. Jothiramalingam, I.A.S., Mrs. Kalpa Rajesh, M. Kandasamy, R. Kantharaj, Krishna Kishore, V. C. Kumaran, M. Kuruvan, Madhu, Malathi Gerard, V Manikesi., M. S. Manjunath, Mary Okelo, M. B. Meti, Dr. K. Nakkiran, K. K. Namboodri, O. P. Narang, P. Narayana Bhat, M. Nellaiappan. Sr. Nicola Sprenger, Nigel Fernandes, Patrick D'Souza, Dr. Pius K. Okela (late), K. Pon Pandian, Poornima Suresh, Fr. Pradeep Sequira, Prahalad N. Kalra, Prakash Gangaram, Quadsia Gandhi, I.A.S., Radhakrishnan, Rajasekaran Nair, Rajesh K. Padia, Rajiv Beri, E Ravichandran, J. N. Reddy, Reinhard Sprenger, Fr. Ronnie Prabhu, Shail M. M., Mrs. Shaila George, Shanmugha Verma, Shiva Kumar, Simen Lourds, Sonia Paul, Steven Pinto, R. Sundar Raj, Surinder Paul, D. Thankaraj, I.A.S., Velmurugan, S. Venkataramani, M. Vijaya Kumar, Vincent A. Pinto, Yesudasan Mories.

I am highly indebted to my wife A. Antoniammal, my children and their spouses, Dr. Denis, Freeda, Prakash, Rupa, Sheela, Peter and my grandchildren Nikita, Alan and Preethika for their unstinted support and cooperation in my literary pursuit.

Dr. G. Francis Xavier Ph. D.

1
DEVELOP HUMILITY

There was an old man in Kerala (India), noted for his serene temperament. Nothing could disturb his calm, not even the gravest provocation. He had in fact become a curiosity for everybody in the village.

One day a few young pranksters decided that they would make him angry. They caught hold of a ruffian, instructed him what to do, and promised to pay him Rs. 500 if he got the old man to lose his cool.

The old man used to have a bath in the river every morning. The youngsters went and hid themselves amidst the scrub on the river bank. When the old man was returning from the river, the young ruffian went up to him and spat on his face. The old man just smiled, and went back to have another dip in the river. When he emerged from the river a second time, the ruffian again spat on his face. Again, the old man smiled and went back for another dip.

More than a hundred times the shocking incident was repeated. Ultimately, the young ruffian was frustrated and stopped the despicable act. In a spirit of genuine repentance, he prostrated before the old man and sought his pardon. The youngsters, too, came out of their hiding and asked for the old man's pardon.

One youngster, who could not believe that a man could exhibit this amount of patience, asked the old man. "Sir, how could you tolerate the atrocious action of that ruffian?"

The old man replied calmly...

QUESTIONS

1. What is the old man's reply?

2. What is the implication of this story?

Check with our answers only after you have tried to come up with your own.

ANSWERS

1. After all he is a child.

2. We love children. We forgive their mischief and continue to show them affection. Similarly if we are able to show love and affection to each and everybody in this world there would be no occasion for us to get angry or irritated. To reach this state of tolerance is not easy. It needs constant practice and diligence.

Author's Note

I read this story some thirty years ago in Swami Shivanand's book "Concentration and Meditation." This has had a lasting impact on me. It has helped me to retain my equanimity in many a trying situation.

2
PLAY THE RIGHT ROLE IN LIFE

A military commander's three-year-old daughter was a bundle of joy and energy. The commander was noted for his strict sense of discipline. One day, annoyed with the child's antics, the mother commented to the father: "What is the use of your being a disciplinarian. Look at your daughter, so naughty and mischievous! Why don't you infuse a little discipline in her?"

The commander took this seriously. He called his daughter and said to her. "Today onwards you should be well-disciplined."

She said, "OK, Daddy!"

"Don't call me Daddy. Whenever you want to talk to me you should begin with the word 'Sir' and also end with the word 'Sir'".

The girl immediately responded. "Sir, yes, sir."

Even if she wanted to have ice cream she had to say "Sir, I want ice cream, sir."

One day the commander went shopping and the little girl wanted to go along with him. He agreed to take her provided she sat in the back seat of the car. She agreed and when they had travelled half the way to their destination, he felt a little hand on the back of his neck and he heard her say...

QUESTIONS

1. What did the little girl say?

2. What is the implication of this story?

Check with our answers only after you have tried to come up with your own.

ANSWERS

1. "Sir, I love you sir." The commander got the message.

2. For the little girl, he is not a military commander but an affectionate father; for his wife, a devoted husband; for his sister, a lovable brother; for his parents, a dutiful son. He can be the military commander only when on duty and amongst his men.

Author's Note

We play a variety of roles in life, depending on the situation and the people with whom we interact. But if we keep thinking of only one role, all the time and at all places then life will become difficult. We should learn to adapt to different roles. Then only life will be easy.

3
OFFER UNIQUE GIFT TO YOUR LOVED ONES

When Jimmy Carter was President of USA, he once had some misunderstanding with his wife. Punctuality was almost an obsession with Carter. because of his naval training.

Rosalyn, his wife, was punctual, though not up to his exacting standards. All too frequently, a deviation of five minutes or even less in their departure time would lead to an exchange of bitter words. For 38 years, it had been the most persistent cause of dissension between them.

On 18th August 1984, Carter went into his study early in the morning to work on a speech and tuned on the radio for the news. When he heard what the date was, he realized it was Rosalyn's birthday and he had not bought her a gift. Now he had no time to buy the gift. All of a sudden, he thought of doing something special without a gift.

QUESTIONS

1. What did Jimmy Carter do for his wife's birthday?

2. What is the implication of this story?

Check with our answers only after you have tried to come up with your own.

ANSWERS

1.   He hurriedly wrote a note that was long overdue. "Happy birthday! As proof of my love, I will never again make an unpleasant comment about your tardiness." He signed it, and delivered it in an envelope, with a kiss. It is reported that till this day he has been keeping his promise and it turned out to be one of the nicest birthday presents in their married life.

2   Learn to think unconventionally. Display your creativity in as many situations as possible. The more we try, the more creative we can become. Why don't you make your next birthday gift to any of your dearest as novel and unique as was done by Jimmy Carter?

4
BEWARE OF DEVIL'S TOOL

A man had a very interesting dream. It was an exhibition held in hell under the supervision of Lucifer. The man was fascinated by the tools used by the devils in their nefarious activities of tempting human beings to commit a variety of sins.

The tools were labelled: Anger, Irritation, Malice, Hatred, Jealousy, Deceit, Sensuality, etc. In a special glass-case, on rich red velvet, rested a worn-out looking tool that seemed harmless. The man asked the demonstrator what it was.

"That tool is Discouragement" whispered the demonstrator

"But why has it been displayed as the show-piece of this exhibition?" he asked. "It looks so harmless and inefficient compared with the others."

A fiendish grin spread over the devil's face as he explained:

QUESTIONS

1. What was the devil's explanation?
2. What is the implication of the story?

Check with our answers only after you have tried to come up with your own.

ANSWERS

1.   "That tool is the secret of our success. It looks so harmless and innocent, but properly used it can take even a saint off his guard."

2.   One word of discouragement is sufficient for some to give up the effort to achieve something great in life. When you hear something discouraging about you, think of this story and visualize how the devils use this tool of discouragement to achieve their objectives. Consider the person using this tool as a devil.

5
ACCEPT UPS AND DOWNS IN LIFE

A king ordered the smith: "Prepare for me a signet with a motto that would temper my happiness when I enjoy good fortune, and lift me in spirit when I am despondent."

The workman had no difficulty making the signet, but the motto part was a tough one.

So he went to a sage and asked, "What can I put on the signet that will temper the king's ecstasy and at the same time lift him when he feels depressed?"

The sage gave him an inscription that fulfilled the king's requirement.

QUESTIONS

1. What was the inscription given by the sage?
2. What is the implication of this story?

Check with our answers only after you have tried to come up with your own.

ANSWERS

1. The sage said, "Inscribe upon the ring: THIS TOO SHALL PASS. When the king gazes upon it in triumph, it will humble his pride. When he looks at it in despair, it will lift his hope."

2.   Toss a coin a hundred times. You will find that the chance of getting heads or tails will be almost equal, with marginal variation. The same holds good in life. Ups and downs are common phenomena. Accept it.

6
THE UNUSUAL WAY TO REACH 'SAMADHI'

Major Soundarajan, an actor in Tamil Nadu (India), had to play the role of a condemned prisoner in a film. The actor wanted to make it a real-life portrayal. So he decided to observe a condemned prisoner. He approached Gunasekar, Superintendent of Vellore Central Jail, and asked his permission to observe a condemned prisoner. The Superintendent agreed. There was a prisoner to be hanged the next day. The Superintendent took the actor to the cell where the prisoner was in solitary confinement.

QUESTIONS

1. Can you guess what the condemned prisoner was doing?

2. What is the moral of this story?

Check with our answers only after you have tried to come up with your own.

ANSWERS

1. He was happily singing in praise of Lord Murugan (one of the deities in Tamil Nadu).

2. The actor could not believe that a condemned man could sing with pleasure hours before his death. He commented to the Superintendent that this fellow was

behaving peculiarly. If he were to act in the movie in this way people would throw stones at him.

The Superintendent said, "What you see as peculiar is not so at all. This is how all the condemned prisoners behave"

(i) "Any person who is awarded capital punishment by the court is given a chance to send a mercy petition to the President of India. At times it takes months for the disposal of the mercy petition. In the meantime the condemned prisoner will be terribly tense awaiting the result of his petition. If the mercy petition is accepted, the person's sentence is commuted to life imprisonment. But if the mercy petition is rejected and the date is fixed for hanging and the prisoner informed of it, all his expectation and anxiety are gone. His death is now certain and that takes him to a different state of consciousness. In yogic lore this would be called 'samadhi', a state of the mind where there is no desire. This is the state of bliss. The force of circumstances brings the condemned prisoner to this state of mind."

(ii) People are afraid of death and do not wish to face it. Though death is a certainty, no one believes in his heart of hearts that he has to die some day.

Author's Note

I have been teaching Yoga to thousands of people and have been explaining the state of Samadhi which is the eighth step in 'Ashtanga' Yoga of Patanjali Maharishi. After hearing this story I could understand clearly the concept of 'Samadhi'".

7
DISPLAY LOVE THROUGH COURAGE

Weisberg, a town in Germany, has an old tower which crowns the fort and bears the name. "The Faith of Women". It is said that Emperor Conard II besieged the fort, and its garrison surrendered with the condition that the women should be allowed to carry away with them their choicest possessions. The Emperor expected that they would carry with them their jewels and such treasures as women are fond of. Imagine his surprise, when standing at the head of his army awaiting their exit, he saw every one of them carrying.

QUESTIONS

1. What were the possessions carried by the women?

2. What is the implication of this story?

Check with our answers only after you have tried to come up with your own.

ANSWERS

1. They carried a husband, a son or a daughter, a brother, or a lover upon their shoulders.

2. It is commonly believed that women are fond of jewels and other valuables. But in times of emergencies

their valued possessions could be none other than their own husbands and children. Love and affection towards one another can never be measured. This can be felt only in a crisis.

8
THE WILL TO LIVE

A disciple was keen to renounce the world but he claimed that his family loved him too much to let him go.

"Love?" said his guru. "That isn't love at all. Listen…" And he revealed a yogic secret to the disciple whereby he could simulate the state of death. The next day the man died for all outward appearances and the entire family was weeping and wailing.

The guru then showed up and told the weeping members that he had the power to bring the man back to life if someone is prepared to die instead. He asked "Any volunteers?"

To the "corpse's" astonishment every member of the family gave a reason why it was necessary to keep his or her own life. His wife said,…

QUESTIONS

1. What was the wife's statement?

2. What is the implication of this story?

Check with our answers only after you have tried to come up with your own.

ANSWERS

1. "There's no need for anyone to die instead. We'll manage without him."

2. The will to live and the urge to survive, at any cost, are strong in every one of us. To face death is not easy.

By and large, everyone is selfish. It is pointless to expect others to sacrifice their lives.

9
BE A GENIUS IN HUMAN RELATIONSHIP

A boy was born to a couple after eleven years of married life. They were a loving couple and the boy was the apple of their eye.

One morning, when the boy was around two years old, the husband saw a medicine bottle open. He was late for his office so he asked his wife to cap the bottle and keep it in the cupboard. The wife, preoccupied with work in the kitchen, totally forgot the matter. The boy playfully went up to the medicine bottle and fascinated by its colour, drank it all. It happened to be a poisonous medicine meant for adults to be consumed in small doses. When the child showed signs of poisoning the wife took him to the hospital, where he died.

The mother was stunned. She was terrified how to face her husband.

When the distraught husband came to the hospital and saw the dead child, he looked at his wife and uttered just four words.

QUESTIONS

1. What were the four words?
2. What is the implication of this story?

Check with our answers only after you have tried to come up with your own.

ANSWERS

1. The husband just said, "I love you darling".

2. The husband's totally unexpected reaction is called proactive behaviour. He is indeed a genius in human relationship. The child is dead. It can never come back to life. There is no point in finding fault with the wife. She also has lost her only child. What she needed at that moment was consolation and sympathy from her husband. That is what he gave her. If everyone can look at life with this kind of perspective, there would be much fewer problems in the world.

Author's Note

I invariably tell this story in all my programmes on Personality Development with particular reference to interpersonal relationship.

10
DON'T GAMBLE

A peon in a bank, noted for his honesty and sincerity, was entrusted with the task of counting the currency notes and bundling them. He wanted to amass wealth. It would have gone against his grain to be dishonest. So he began to purchase lottery tickets and waited for lady luck to smile on him. He visited temples and prayed for a bumper prize. But not even a consolation prize came his way. He blamed God for not listening to his prayer.

One morning, there was a surprise in store for him. Lying at his door was a sack full of 500 rupee notes. Overnight he had become a multi-millionaire.

When his delight at this sudden windfall subsided, he took a 500-rupee note, gave it to his wife and said. "Let's have a grand breakfast. No need to cook. Order something from the hotel." While she was away to arrange for the breakfast, he sat down and wrote his resignation letter to the bank.

His wife did not return even an hour later. When she finally returned, she reported that all the hotels in the town were closed. His son, who had gone to the bank with the resignation letter, came and reported that the bank manager had resigned his job and his son was asked to hand over the resignation letter to the Assistant

Manager, who had not come to work.

QUESTIONS

1. What could be the reason that all the hotels were closed?

2. Why did the manager resign his post?

3. What is the implication of this story?

Check with our answers only after you have tried to come up with your own.

ANSWERS

1. & 2 Everyone in that town-including the hotel owner, the hotel employees and the bank staff got one sack full of 500-rupee notes. They did not wish to work anymore.

3. In real life, everyone wants to have more pay and more facilities without a corresponding increase in the production of goods and services. The result is inflation. Money is nothing but an exchange instrument for goods and services.

11
PRODUCE QUALITY GOODS

A company, dealing in dog food, was holding its annual sales convention. The sales personnel were brimming with ideas. The advertising director introduced a point-of-sales scheme that would "revolutionize the industry". The sales director extolled the virtues of "the best damn sales force in the business." Finally it was time for the president to go to the podium and make his closing remarks.

"Over the past few days", he began, "We've heard from all our division heads their wonderful plans for the coming year. Now we draw to a close, I have only one question. If we have the best advertising, the best marketing strategy, the best sales force, how come we sell less dog food than anyone else in the business?"

There was pin-drop silence in the convention hall. Finally, after what seemed like forever, a weak voice answered from the back of the room.

QUESTIONS

1. What was the answer from the back of the room?
2. What is the implication of this story?

Check with our answers only after you have tried to come up with your own.

ANSWERS

1. "Because dogs hate it."

2. Don't overlook the obvious. See the underlying cause from every angle. For effective sale of any product the quality of the product should be given maximum priority.

12
LOVE CAN BIND MORE FIERCELY THAN COMPULSION

During the early days of the nineteenth century a wealthy plantation owner was moved by the heartbreaking sobs of a slave girl who was about to step into the auction block to be sold. Obviously she was not very happy to be sold as a slave. Moved by a momentary impulse of compassion, he bought her at a very high price and then disappeared into the crowd.

When the auction was over, the clerk came to the sobbing girl and handed her bill of sale. To her astonishment, the unknown plantation owner had written "Free" on the paper. She stood speechless, as one by one the other slaves were claimed by their owners and dragged away. Suddenly, she threw herself at the feet of the clerk and exclaimed, "Where is the man who bought me? I must find him! He has set me free!" and further continued,…

QUESTIONS

1. What did she say further to the clerk?
2. What is the implication of this story?

Check with our answers only after you have tried to come up with your own.

ANSWERS

1. "I must serve him as long as I live!"

2. The gesture of compassion showed by the plantation owner made the girl willing to become a lifelong slave to him. Love can bind more fiercely than compulsion and coercion.

13
KNOW THE TRUTH

One day a disciple found a glittering object on the road. He took the precious object, showed it to the master and asked him, "Is this a genuine diamond?"

The master was supposed to be very knowledgeable about gems. He instructed the disciple, "Go to the library and read all about diamonds." The disciple went, studied everything about diamonds and returned after having acquired sufficient knowledge about diamonds.

On his return the master said, "I can now tell you that the stone that you picked up on the wayside was a genuine diamond."

"How strange", asked the disciple. "Why did you not tell me that before? Is there any reason for that?"

"Yes", the Master answered,...

QUESTIONS

1.   What was the master's answer?

2.   What is the implication of this story?

Check with our answers only after you have tried to come up with your own.

ANSWERS

1. "It is my firm conviction that you should not be gullible. You have to test everything personally. Now that you have acquired the knowledge about diamonds, you can verify whether what I told you is correct. Whether with precious gems or with life you are quite capable of being your own expert."

2. No one knows the truth better than you, provided you know what it means to live with the true You.

14
DON'T CLAIM OMNISCIENCE

Once a pundit wrote a long poem in praise of the king. The king was much pleased and offered him precious gems and gold. As an additional honour, he ordered his men to take the Pundit to his village in a palanquin with pomp and show.

As the troupe was passing through a village with the sound of trumpets, a young cowherd curiously asked one of the palanquin bearers, "What are you carrying?"

The man replied "Punditji".

"Who is a Punditji?"

"A learned person."

"Who is a learned person?"

"A man who knows everything."

"Does he really know everything?"

In the meantime the whole procession had come to a halt. Punditji peeped out of the palanquin and irritably asked. "Why have you people stopped?"

One of the men said, "Punditji, here is a boy who is asking questions that we cannot answer."

The puffed up Pundit then came down from the palanquin and said, "Is that so? What question do you have?"

The boy bent down and drew disjointed zigzag lines on the ground with his stick. Then he looked up and asked," Can you tell what this is?"

The Pundit could not. It did not resemble an alphabet of any language he knew. It did not look like a snake or a rope because the lines were disjointed.

The boy started laughing and said, "What Punditji! Don't you know such a simple thing?" The Pundit had to concede defeat. He said to the boy, "All right, you tell the answer." The boy answered...

QUESTIONS

1. What was the boy's answer?
2. What is the implication of this story?

ANSWERS

1. "This is how my bullock passes urine"
2. No one can claim to possess total knowledge. The story is also a pointer to the modern trend of specialization. The boy knew only about cattle and the Pundit knew about what he had learnt in his lifetime. Acknowledging the inadequacy of our knowledge would motivate us to gain greater knowledge in our field of interest.

Author's Note

This story was related to me by my grandfather when I was studying in fifth standard.

15
ACCOMPLISH UNBELIEVABLE FEETS THROUGH FAITH

On the bank of a river lived a hermit. Over thirty years he had been doing 'Sadhana' to walk on water. He was a great devotee of Lord Krishna. He subsisted only on cow's milk, which was supplied by a girl of eleven years, living on the other bank of the river.

One day her mother told her, "There are heavy clouds. There is going to be a downpour and the river will be flooded. Tell the hermit that you won't be able to supply milk to him tomorrow."

The girl did so.

The hermit told the girl, "Don't worry about the flood. I will teach you a 'mantra' and you can walk on water. Close your eyes and repeat 'Krishna, Krishna, Krishna', and you can comfortably walk on water."

As expected the rain came in torrent and the river was in spate. The girl got ready to take milk to the hermit. The mother refused. But the girl persisted and told her that the hermit had given her a 'mantra' to walk on water. Believing her, the mother allowed her to go. The girl went to the river closed her eyes, repeated "Krishna, Krishna, Krishna", and she walked on water. The hermit was looking on in wonder.

The girl returned home, repeating the 'mantra', walking on water.

The hermit thought to himself, "How wonderful. I enabled that girl to walk on water. I have the power. Now let me try for myself."

Confidently he stepped on water and drowned forthwith.

QUESTION

What is the implication of this story?

Check with our answer only after you have tried to come up with your own.

ANSWER

Faith can move mountains. The young girl had tremendous faith in the mantra given by the hermit, but not the hermit himself. It is implicit faith that can do wonders in this world. All great scientists had this kind of faith that nature had something to reveal and they brought forth unbelievable scientific truths for us to enjoy in the modern world in the form of radio, telephone, television, tape recorder, computer, airplane and what else. All these inventions were born out of implicit faith.

16
DEVELOP PURITY IN HEART

Two monks on a pilgrimage came to a river bank. There they saw a girl dressed in all her finery and obviously not knowing how to cross the river.

Without much ado, one of the monks took her on his back, carried her across, and put her down on dry ground.

Then the monks continued their walk. But the other monk started complaining. "Surely it is not right to touch a woman; it is against the commandments to have close contact with women; how can you go against the rules for the monks?"

The complainant bemoaned endlessly. The monk who carried the girl walked along silently, but finally he remarked,...

QUESTIONS

1.   What was the monk's remark?
2.   What is the implication of this story?

Check with our answers only after you have tried to come up with your own.

ANSWERS

1.   "I let her down by the river. But why are you still carrying her?"

2. Any kind of action done with an immaculate heart can never be sinful.

17
WORK SHARPER, NOT HARDER

A hard-working young man was engaged to cut trees in a forest.

On the first day he felled seven trees in eight hours. The next day he managed to fell only five, though he worked for eight hours. On the third day he could fell only three trees. On the fourth day the number of trees felled came down to one.

Puzzled about his deteriorating performance, he sought the advice of his boss. The boss asked him a simple question.

QUESTIONS

1. What was the question?
2. Why was the return on his labour diminishing?
3. What is the moral of this story?

Check with your answers only after you have tried to come up with your own.

ANSWERS

1. "Did you sharpen your axe?" The young man answered "No".

2. The blunt axe was giving less return on his labour.

3. WORK SHARPER, NOT HARDER. This is an essential principle of Time Management. To get worthwhile results one should work in an organized manner.

18
HANDICAP—A SPUR TO ACCOMPLISHMENT

An Athenian was lame on one foot. He was ridiculed by his fellow soldiers because of his lameness. He gave them a fitting reply thus:...

QUESTIONS

1. What was his reply?
2. What is the moral of this story?

Check with our answers only after you have tried to come up with your own.

ANSWERS

1. "I am here to fight, not to run."

2. The greatest problem confronted by handicapped persons is an inferiority complex and not the handicap as such. They need to be imbued with confidence if they are to achieve. The soldier was able to overcome this complex. He was very confident of his ability to fight.

19
A SPECIAL MESSAGE FOR YOUNGSTERS

A trainee psychologist was visiting a mental hospital. A resident doctor of the place took him round.

In one corner, they found an inmate rocking back and forth in a chair, mumbling agitatedly, "Lulu, Lulu, Lulu,...."

"What brought this man here?" the psychologist asked the doctor.

"It is a very sad story", the doctor explained. "This man was in deep love with a girl called Lulu and she jilted him."

The psychologist tentatively concluded that failure in love would lead to insanity.

In another block of the hospital, the doctor and his companion came across another inmate banging his head repeatedly against the wall and mourning, "Lulu, Lulu, Lulu,..."

The psychologist was aghast. He commented, "Poor fellow, another victim of Lulu. She must have been very pretty and jilted many men I suppose."

The doctor answered,...

QUESTIONS

1.   What was the doctor's answer?

2.   What is the implication of this story?

Check with our answers only after you have tried to come up with your own.

ANSWERS

1.   "Oh, you are wrong there. This is the man who married Lulu."

2.   Youngsters must make a special note of this story. It is natural to fall in love during adolescence. But if one is not able to marry the person with whom one has fallen in love, it is not the end of the world. Life has much greater meaning than romance and marriage.

20
THE BEST ANTIDOTE
FOR WORRY

The only son of a mother had died on the war front. World War II was then raging and matters had to be done with speed. A neighbour was informed and requested to convey the distressing news to the mother.

The neighbour gathered a few friends, and went over to her house. She was on her hands and knees scrubbing the kitchen floor. The man said quietly, "I have something very sad to tell you." Then he paused. "Bill has been killed in France."

The mother hesitated just for a moment, then the brush continued going around and around. Finally she said, "Well, all of you sit down, won't you please? I'll make you a cup of tea."

They protested, but she insisted. "Please", she said "I want to make you some tea! I feel like doing it." And she chatted as she boiled the water, brought out some cakes, arranged the tea, and sat down with the callers.

A long time after the mourning period was over, her neighbour said to her, "I've always admired you for the way you took the news of your boy's death. But I have never been able to understand it."

"Well" she said, "my grandmother once told me:...

QUESTIONS

1. What did her grandmother tell her?

2. What is the implication of this story?

Check with our answers only after you have tried to come up with your own.

ANSWERS

1. "Whenever you get any distressing news, don't stop your work. Whatever you are supposed to be doing at that moment, you should continue to do."

2. The best antidote for worry and anxiety is work.

21
ACCEPT THE INEVITABLE DEATH

Kisa Gotami's only son died. Though grief-stricken, she carried the dead child to all her neighbours, asking for medicine, and the people said, "She has lost her senses. The boy is dead."

At last Kisa Gotami met a man who replied to her request, "I cannot give you medicine for your child, but I know a physician who can."

The woman said, "Pray tell me, Sir, who is it?" and the man replied, "Go to Sakyamuni the Buddha."

She then approached the Buddha with all hope and confidence and cried, "Lord and Master, give me the medicine that will make my boy come to life."

The Buddha promised to help her provided she would bring a handful of mustard seeds. The woman was extremely happy at this condition and was hastening to procure what he wanted. But the Buddha added a rider,...

QUESTIONS

1. What was the rider to the Buddha's condition?

2. Was the woman able to fulfill it?

3. What is the implication of this story?

Check with our answers only after you have tried to come up with your own.

ANSWERS

1. Lord Buddha said, "The mustard seed must be taken from a house where no one has lost a child, husband, parent or friend."

2. Kisa Gotami went from house to house, and the people pitied her and said, "Here is mustard seed; take it! But when she asked, "Has a son or a daughter, a father or a mother, ever died in your family?" They answered her, "Alas! The living are few, but the dead are many. Do not remind us of our lost ones." And there was no house where some beloved one had not died.

3. To the desolate woman the realization came that a lamp lives when men flicker up and gets extinguished again. She considered the fate of men, and thought to herself, "How selfish am I in my grief!" Death is common to all; yet for one who has surrendered all acts of selfishness, there is a path that leads him to immortality.

22
PARADOX OF MOTHER'S LOVE

A young mother takes her six-year old child on an outing to the zoo. In the beginning, all is light-hearted joy as they walk hand in hand in the delightful evening sunlight. Then the little boy, suddenly slipping away from her, gets lost in the crowd. After half an hour of agonizing search, she finds him not fallen into the cage of a lion as she dreaded, but ecstatically watching the sea-lions: Her earlier feeling of relief turns to one of anger and she slaps him. His bliss is at once transformed into furious resentment; he bursts into tears.

Repentant, she buys the child an ice-cream cone and his resentment magically changes into pleasure. Once more they love each other. But then he wants another cone. She refuses, it would spoil his supper. He gets into fits of rage. Once more they are angry. After half a dozen or so such incidents and worn out by their extreme feelings of love and anger, they take the bus home. He is sleepy and his head trustfully rests on her shoulder. All… again.

QUESTIONS

1. Fill in the blank.

2. What is the implication of this story?

Check with our answers only after you have tried to come up with your own.

ANSWERS

1. Love.

2. This is an example of how a person can be angry without being in anger. Though the mother showed her anger and even slapped her son, it is not due to bitterness of heart but out of passionate love for him. That is life—a continuous process of anger, love, emotional upset and ecstasy.

23
LIBERATE FROM UNDESIRABLE HABITS

Two men got drunk on an island. About midnight, they staggered down to their little boat, took up the oars and started to row. They should have reached the main land within an hour but daybreak saw them in the island, still rowing.

QUESTIONS

1. Why were they not able to reach the mainland?

2. What is the implication of this story?

Check with our answers only after you have tried to come up with your own.

ANSWERS

1. They did not untie the rope that secured the boat to the shore.

2. As long as we are tied up with negative thoughts and habits, we cannot attain freedom and happiness.

24
MOTIVATION—THE KEY TO SUCCESS

Lou Little was the football coach at Georgetown University. Their college president came to him one day and said, "Do you know Harold Chapman?" "Sure", Lou answered"He has been on my squad for years. He is an average player. The problem is that he is not well motivated."

"Well", the president continued, "we just received a message that his father died. Will you break the news to him?"

The coach put his arm around Chapman and told him the sad news. "I'm sorry, son, you take a week off."

But the next day Chapman was in the locker room preparing for the game. "What are you doing here?" the coach inquired in amazement.

"Today is the big game. I have got to play", he replied.

"But you know I have not included you in the team."

"Include me and you won't be sorry", the moist-eyed player said very firmly.

The coach softened and decided that if he won the toss he would use him for the first play. He would not do much damage on the kickoff return. Georgetown won the toss.

During the game, Harold came tearing down the field with the ball, like a tornado. The coach, pleasantly shocked, used him in another play and then another. He blocked; he tacked; he passed; he ran. He literally won the ball game for Georgetown University that day.

In the locker room the coach, perplexed, asked, "Son, what happened?" The player said...

QUESTIONS

1. What was the boy's answer?

2. What is the implication of this story?

Check with our answers only after you have tried to come up with your own.

ANSWERS

1. "My father was blind. Only today he witnessed my game."

2. Motivation provides stimulus. He believed that his father would see his game after his death. This belief motivated him to play exceedingly well.

25
PATIENCE PAYS IN THE ULTIMATE

During the reign of Queen Elizabeth, Dr. Thomas Cooper edited a learned dictionary adding 33,000 words, and imparting many other improvements. He had already spent eight years in collecting material for his edition. His wife was a woman of little understanding.

One day she went into his library and burnt every note he had prepared due to fear that he would kill himself with study.

The doctor shortly after coming in and seeing the destruction, inquired who had done it. His wife boldly answered that she had. The patient man heaved a deep sigh and said, "Oh Dinah, Dinah, thou hast given me a world of trouble!"

QUESTIONS

1. What did he do then?
2. What is the implication of this story?

Check with our answers only after you have tried to come up with your own.

ANSWERS

1. Then he quietly sat down to another eight years

of hard labour, to replace the notes which she had destroyed.

2.   The astounding patience shown by Dr Thomas Cooper becomes possible if the heart is without rancour and the character is strong.

26
ELICIT COOPERATION

The chairman of an automobile company was confronted with the necessity of infusing enthusiasm into a discouraged and disorganized group of automobile salesmen. Calling a sales meeting, he urged his men to tell him exactly what they expected from him. As they talked, he wrote their ideas on the blackboard. He then said, "I'll give you all these qualities you expect from me. Now I want you to tell me what I rightfully can expect from you?"

QUESTIONS

1. What was the response of the salesmen?
2. What is the implication of this story?

Check with our answers only after you have tried to come up with your own.

ANSWERS

1. The replies from the salesmen came thick and fast: loyalty, honesty, initiative, optimism, team work, and eight hours a day of enthusiastic work. One man volunteered to work fourteen hours a day. The meeting ended with added strength and new-found inspiration and in course of time, the sales increased phenomenally.

2. The methodology used by the chairman was unique. Instead of commanding the salesmen to do this and that, he volunteered to fulfill their needs first and thereby elicited their cooperation to do what he wanted them to do.

27
BE GENEROUS AND PHILANTHROPIC

There lived a rich landlord in England in the twelfth century. He had little compassion for the poor. His wife was generous and sympathetic towards the poor. When her health failed and she was about to die, she requested her husband to give something to the poor every year in her memory.

Setting fire to a branch, he told her he would donate the produce from as much land as she could crawl around while the branch still burned.

QUESTIONS

1. What did the woman do?
2. What is the implication of this story?

ANSWERS

1. Despite her weakened condition, she crawled around twenty-three acres of land before the flame died out. Touched by her love for the needy, her husband kept his word.

2. Some 800 years after her death, the magnanimity of the English woman for the poor continues to have its effects. To this day, as a result of her remarkable bequest,

a supply of six pounds of flour is given to each adult and three pounds to each child in two small Hampshire villages.

Humanity continues to survive because of such generous and philanthropic souls in this world.

28
DISPEL DARKNESS THROUGH LOVE

The Master asked his disciples, "How do you recognize when the night ends and the day begins?"

One disciple answered, "When I am able to distinguish between a cow and a horse."

Another answered, "When I can differentiate between a neem tree and a mango tree."

The Master said, "No." Then he proceeded with his answer.

QUESTIONS

1. What was the Master's answer?
2. What is the implication of this story?

Check with our answers only after you have tried to come up with your own.

ANSWERS

1. "When you can recognize everyone as your brothers and sisters."

2. Darkness goes and light comes only when a person is able to show love and affection to people.

29
THE PRAYER THAT GOD IS PLEASED WITH

A cobbler and a priest died. The cobbler was hard working, totally immersed in his work all the time. The priest spent most of his time in prayer and meditation, and was venerated for his piety and holiness.

Both the souls went to the Pearly Gate of Heaven. The cobbler was admitted immediately into heaven while the priest was asked to wait.

The priest waited for some time and was becoming irritable. He complained to St. Peter, who was guarding the heavenly gate: "How is it that you admitted the cobbler immediately into heaven? He never attended church services and never prayed. I, who had spent most of my time in prayer and contemplation, have been asked to wait, is this fair?"

St. Peter answered: "You are wrong. The cobbler did pray to the Lord with only one sentence everyday before going to bed. Our Lord was much pleased with his one-sentence prayer."

QUESTIONS

1. Can you guess the cobbler's prayer?
2. What is the implication of this story?

Check with our answers only after you have tried to come up with your own.

ANSWERS

1. "Oh Lord, I had no time to pray. Please forgive me."

2. Sincerity is regarded more valuable in the spiritual realm than mere rituals and prayer.

30
PORTRIAT OF GOD AND SATAN

A young and famous painter decided to create a truly great portrait, a lively one full of the joy of God, a portrait of a man whose eyes radiated eternal peace. After a long hunt, he came across a shepherd with shining eyes in a remote village. One look was enough to convince him that God was present in this young man. The artist painted his picture and millions of copies were sold.

After some twenty years, the artist decided to paint another portrait, that of Satan. His experience had shown that life is not all goodness and Satan also exists in man. After a long search he met a prisoner in a jail. The man had committed seven murders and was sentenced to be hanged. His face was the ugliest that he could find on earth. It perfectly portrayed devilish demeanour. The artist began to paint this portrait and when he was about to complete it, the artist saw the prisoner sobbing bitterly.

QUESTIONS

1. Why did the prisoner weep bitterly?

2. What is the implication of this story?

Check with our answers only after you have tried to come up with your own.

ANSWERS

1.   The prisoner was the same young man whom the artist had painted as the one radiating eternal peace. A girl from a very affluent family had fallen in love with his looks and demeanour and married him. The sudden wealth had led him into all kinds of vices. He squandered his inheritance and took to crime.

2.   Beautify your life with inner glow than with outer show.

31
REAL CONTRIBUTION COMES FROM THE POOR

As the children were playing on the beach, a ragged woman was going around now and then picking something from the beach. Whenever she came across a child she would smile and greet the child. But the parents told their picnicking children to keep away from the old woman because she was dirty and poor.

QUESTIONS

1. What was the old woman doing?

2. What is the implication of this story?

ANSWERS

1. The old woman was picking up any broken glass on the beach so that the children should not injure themselves.

2. In any society, the real contribution is made mostly by the poorer sections. They have a natural inclination to come to the rescue of people in trouble. For example, in an accident, the poor people working nearby will rush to rescue of the accident victims; but the rich people, travelling in their cars, will not bother even to look at the victims.

32
FAITH CAN MOVE MOUNTAINS

An old woman regularly read the Bible before retiring at night. One day she came across the following passage:

"If you have faith as little as a mustard seed and ask the mountain to go away, it will go."

She decided to test the efficacy of this passage. There was a hillock behind her house. She commanded the hillock to go away from there and went to bed.

In the morning she got up as usual and remembered her command to the hillock. She wore her spectacles and peered through the window. The hillock was there. Then she muttered to herself,...

QUESTIONS

1. What did she mutter to herself?
2. What is the implication of this story?

Check with our answers only after you have tried to come up with your own.

ANSWERS

1. "Ah! That's what I thought."
2. What she thought was that the mountain would not go. While her outer mind gave the command, her

inner mind was convinced that she was giving a futile order. She did not have even an atom of faith in her command.

33
ARGUMENTS ARE FUTILE

Everyday, a hawker of hand-fans passed by the Zamindar's house. Invariably he bragged about the unique and wonderful fans he sold. No one, he claimed, had ever seen such fans before.

The Zamindar sent for the hawker. He could see that the fans were of inferior quality. The hawker, however, insisted that the fans would last for one hundred years, if used properly. The price he quoted was Rs. 2,000.

Against his better judgment, the Zamindar bought the fan out of curiosity. Within three days the fan began to fall apart and was totally ruined before the week ended.

The furious Zamindar summoned the hawker. The fan-seller said "But Sir, these fans are guaranteed to last one hundred years. It is possible that your Excellency did not use it in the proper manner."

The Zamindar asked, "While selling the fan, why did you not tell me how to use it?"

The hawker replied, "Maharaj, but you did not ask. I presumed that your Excellency knew."

"All right", the Zamindar said, "Now tell me how to use this fan?"

QUESTIONS

1.   Could you guess how the fan was to be used?

2.   What is the implication of this story?

ANSWERS

1.   The fan-seller said, "To use this kind of fan the user must keep the fan steady and move only the head. The fan should not be shaken at all."

2.   Everyone is right from his or her own perspective. Never argue with anyone. Arguments are futile.

34
SHOW ANGER WITHOUT BEING IN ANGER

In a certain village, a cobra bit and killed many people. The villagers complained to a holy man, whom they believed had miraculous powers over animals.

The holy man called the cobra and ordered it not to bite anybody. Thereafter, the cobra entirely ceased its habit of biting people.

But the time came when, because the cobra was quiet and harmless, the villagers started teasing it. Even the small boys pelted stones at it.

The troubled cobra was now resentful of the holy man's command. It went over to him and complained about what was happening.

The holy man was sympathetic. He commented...

QUESTIONS

1. What did the holy man say to the cobra?
2. What is the implication of this story?

Check with our answers only after you have tried to come up with your own.

ANSWERS

1. "I asked you not to bite. Did I tell you not to hiss?"

2. We can show anger without being angry. The best example is the anger we show towards our children. We even beat them, though we are not really angry with them. In the same manner, an employer or an executive may show his anger towards his subordinates without harbouring any feelings of anger.

35
ENJOY WHAT YOU ARE DOING

A gentleman visiting Thomas Alva Edison at Menlo Park, asked him to give a motto to his son who was about to enter business. The great inventor replied, "Well, I will give him this,...

QUESTIONS

1. What was the motto given by Edison?

2. What is the implication of this story?

Check with our answers only after you have tried to come up with your own.

ANSWERS

1. "Never look at the clock."

2. If one enjoys what one is doing, then time passes without his knowledge. Clock watchers are bored with their work. Success eludes them.

36
THE WILL TO LIVE

Looking at the sick man, the doctor decided to tell him the truth.

"I feel I should tell you. You are a very sick man. I'm sure you would like to know the facts. Your end has come. Now, is there anyone you would like to see?"

Bending down toward his patient, the doctor heard him feebly answer, "Yes."

"Who is it?" the doctor asked.

The patient replied,...

QUESTIONS

1. What was the sick man's reply?
2. What is the implication of this story?

Check with our answers only after you have tried to come up with your own.

ANSWERS

1. In a slightly stronger tone, the sick man said, "Another doctor."

2. Death is inevitable, but no one wants to give up hope of survival. Research has proved beyond doubt

that people with the will to live will surmount all kinds of health problems. Dr. Carl Simonton of USA has cured hundreds of cases of terminal cancer patients through meditation techniques. One important aspect to be noted here is that all those patients had a very strong will to live.

37
MAKE EVERY SECOND OF YOUR LIFE A MASTERPIECE

The story of the tortoise and the hare is a familiar one. The two raced but the hare, overconfident, took a nap before running. Whereas the tortoise, without any rest, continuously ran and ultimately won the race.

QUESTION

1.   What is the implication of this story?

Check with our answer only after you have tried to come up with your own.

ANSWER

This story is a typical representation of the modern trend of our race with time. Time is the tortoise and human beings are the hare. Time never stops but we spend our time unproductively. Some men overtake the tortoise until the last hour of life. They are more likely to achieve something great and outstanding in life. Many others do not overtake the tortoise from the start. They are real losers.

Why don't you beat the tortoise commencing today?

38
THE POWER OF SILENCE

When Thomas Alva Edison received an offer from the Western Union Company for the ticker he had invented, he was undecided what price to ask. He requested for a couple of days time to think about the matter. Edison and his wife talked it over thoroughly and Mrs. Edison suggested that he ask for $20,000. Edison thought it an exorbitant figure. But on the appointed day, he went to the Western Union office ready to ask for the amount.

"Well, now, Mr. Edison", the Western Union representative said after he had greeted him. "How much do you want?"

Edison tried to say $20,000, but it still seemed to him an outrageous demand and he could not utter it. He hesitated, and then he stood speechless before the Western Union official. In the quiet that followed, the official waited restlessly for Edison to answer. Still Edison did not speak.

The impatient businessman was unable to tolerate silence of this nature for long. He said "How about...?

QUESTIONS

1. What was the amount quoted by the businessman?

2.   What is the implication of this story?

Check with our answers only after you have tried to come up with your own.

ANSWERS

1.   The businessman quoted a Hundred Thousand Dollars.

2.   Clearly it was Edison who benefited from the silence and the Western Union Company that lost. The company's representative lacked the patience to wait for a reply.

People in business have a tendency to say what they want to say without waiting to listen to the other person. We prefer to conclude business transactions as expeditiously as possible. Listening to silence calls for some patience; many simply cannot remain quiet for long.

39
PROFOUND IMPACT OF ENCOURAGING WORDS

As a child, Walter Scott was considered a dullard. His usual place was a dull corner in the school-room. He sat there with the high pointed paper cap on his head.

The noted poet Robert Burns once visited Walter's house. He noticed a picture under which a couplet was written.

Burns found the couplet fascinating and asked who its author was. No one knew. Timidly Walter Scott rose up and quoted the rest of the poem. Laying his hand on the boy's head, Burns exclaimed,...

QUESTIONS

1. What did Burns say to Walter?

2. What is the implication of this story?

Check with our answers only after you have tried to come up with your own.

ANSWERS

1. "You will be a great man in Scotland some day."

2. Robert Burn's encouraging words motivated Walter Scott to become one of the greatest poets in Scotland. We underestimate youngsters' talents judging from their

academic performance.

The fact is, the marks and grades obtained in schools and colleges are no indicators of their future growth. Further, any kind of genuine appreciation will deeply register in a child's mind and will greatly motivate him.

40
OVERCOME PHYSICAL HANDICAP

One day Hobhouse visited Lord Byron, at his villa near Genoa. Hobhouse was his college friend. While walking in the garden, Byron, conscious of his deformity, suddenly turned to his guest and exclaimed, "Now I know, Hobhouse, you are looking at my foot!"

Hobhouse courteously replied,...

QUESTIONS

1. What was Hobhouse's reply?

2. What is the implication of this story?

Check with our answers only after you have tried to come up with your own.

ANSWERS

1. "My friend Byron, nobody thinks of or looks at anything but your head."

2. Handicapped people have a niggling anxiety that people are conscious of their deformity to the exclusion of all other factors. This affects their life and performance. In reality, people look at their talents more than their physical features. The only way to overcome this complex is to achieve something outstanding in their own fields.

41
FREE GIFT HAS NO VALUE

George Bernard Shaw was browsing at a book-stall selling used books at low prices. Shaw came across a volume containing his own plays. The book was a copy he had gifted to a friend, as on the fly-leaf, G.B.S. had inscribed, "With the compliments of George Bernard Shaw". Buying the book, Shaw wrote under the inscription,…

QUESTIONS

1. What did Shaw write?

2. What is the implication of this story?

Check with our answers only after you have tried to come up with your own.

ANSWERS

1. "With renewed compliments, G.B.S", and sent it back to the earlier recipient.

2. Anything given free has no value.

42
THE WORLD IS A REFLEC-TION OF OUR OWN

Aesop, the famous story teller, was seated by the roadside at a place near Athens. One day a passerby asked him, "What sort of people live in Athens?"

"Please tell me", said Aesop "wherefrom you come and what kind of people live there."

Frowning, the stranger replied, "I come from Argos and the people there are liars, thieves and quarrelsome by nature."

"I am sorry to tell you this", said Aesop. "You will find the people of Athens much the same."

Later, another man appeared and asked Aesop the same question. Aesop inquired wherefrom he came and, the stranger's face lit up with pleasure.

"I come from Argos where people are kind, friendly and thoughtful. I am sorry to have left them."

Then Aesop replied,...

QUESTIONS

1. What was Aesop's reply?

2. What is the implication of this story?

Check with our answers only after you have tried to come up with your own.

ANSWERS

1. "My friend", said Aesop, "I am glad to tell you, you will find the people of Athens much the same."

2. Both came from the same place Argos, but held different opinions. The world is nothing but a reflection of our own thoughts and feelings. A good person will think that everyone is good and a bad person otherwise.

43
HOW TO CONQUER ANGER

Sister Elizabeth Kenny, the famed Irish-Australian nurse managed to stay constantly cheerful, no matter what the provocation was. One day a friend asked her whether this was her inborn quality. She said "No", and continued. "when I was very young, my mother gave me a piece of advice which I have been seriously following."

QUESTIONS

1. What was her mother's advice?

2. What is the implication of this story?

Check with our answers only after you have tried to come up with your own.

ANSWERS

1. "Anyone who angers you conquers you."

2. Anger is our reaction to someone's action or inaction. But our reaction is a matter of our own choice. The best answer to provocation is inner silence.

44
THE UNFAILING MEDICINE

A young intern asked an experienced doctor, "What is the best medicine which can cure all diseases?"

The doctor answered. "The most wonderful medicine is not compounded of rare and expensive drugs. It is the most commonplace thing I know. It is not a drug at all. It consists of four letters.

QUESTIONS

1. What is the four-letter medicine?
2. What is the implication of this story?

ANSWERS

1. "W O R K"

2. When the mind is completely absorbed in creative activity, there is no room for self-pity, depression, worry, anxiety, tension and other negative emotions. In the absence of such negative emotions, the mind becomes calm and that results in robust health.

45
HOW TO BECOME AN ENLIGHTENED SOUL?

The Master was considered an enlightened soul. A visitor from afar came to discover what was special in him. He found nothing extraordinary in him.

"I see nothing unusual about him", he commented.

"Of course, you don't", answered an inmate of the Ashram. "It is a spiritual law that no man can see above his own level. His supremacy exists, but you can't understand it. A rabbit knows nothing about a star."

"I still don't see", the man further declared, "how he is different from others. He walks and talks much like anyone else."

"It's true", the inmate continued. "When he walks and talks, do you know the difference between you and him?"

"What?" he inquired.

The inmate answered,...

QUESTIONS

1. What is the answer of the Ashram in-mate?

2. What is the implication of this story?

Check with our answers only after you have tried to come up with your own.

ANSWERS

1. "You do them mechanically. He does them consciously."

2. Try to understand at a deeper level the difference between mechanical behaviour and conscious action. Make it a point every day, to observe your own behaviour patterns. You will notice that there is a sea-change in your personality for the better.

46
A VALID STATEMENT

Three friends sat on a park bench. Two of them were having a lively argument over religion and philosophy. Each accused the other of being childish and superstitious. They finally turned to the third man to decide who was right.

The third man said, "You would never believe me if I told you."

The others encouraged, "Tell us anyway."

The third man replied,...

QUESTIONS

1. What is the third man's reply?

2. What is the implication of this story?

Check with our answers only after you have tried to come up with your own.

ANSWERS

1. "I am right", said the third man.

"What do you mean?" demanded the other two.

"I don't have to convince you I'm right", the third man asserted.

2. The man who really knows has no compulsion to prove it.

47
HOW TO BECOME A WELL KNOWN WRITER

The novelist Sinclair Lewis was asked to talk to a group of undergraduates at a well known university. All those present had literary ambitions.

"How many of you really want to be writers?" the famous author began.

Every student in the room raised his hand.

"In that case" said the novelist,...

QUESTIONS

1. What did the novelist say to the students?
2. What is the implication of this story?

Check with our answers only after you have tried to come up with your own.

ANSWERS

1. "There is no point in wasting your time here. Go home and write."

2. Choose a specific goal in life. Then plunge into action to fulfill it. Unremitting pursuit of the goals is the only key to great accomplishments. If you want to become an actor/actress, every moment of your wakeful state should be used to develop the art of acting. The same holds good for achieving anything great in life.

48
AS THE PROFESSION, SO THE PROSPERITY

There were plenty of fishes in a lake privately owned by a wealthy merchant. A fisherman, looking for easy game, stole into his premises one night to poach.

The owner, having suspected that someone had trespassed into his property, set his guards to fetch him. The fisherman saw the guards looking for him everywhere with lighted torches.

With some quick imagination, he removed his shirt, smeared himself with ashes, closed his eyes, sat under a nearby tree and pretended to be lost in meditation.

The guards failed to spot the intruder. All they saw was a holy man in deep meditation.

The owner, when he heard of it, was very happy that the holy man had chosen his place as his abode, and went and prostrated before him with his offering of flowers, fruits and money.

The next day word spread that a great sage had taken up residence in the premises of the wealthy merchant. People started pouring in to pay respects to the 'sage' with offerings of flowers, fruits, food and money.

QUESTIONS

1. What did the fisherman do?

2. What is the implication of this story?

Check with our answers only after you have tried to come up with your own.

ANSWERS

1. The fisherman-turned-sage was astounded at his good fortune. "Better to live on the faith of the people as a sage, than to toil with my hand", he mused. He continued to meditate and never went back to work.

2. There is considerable correlation between one's career and what one gets out of it. Who gets more and more money in life? He who continuously deals with money—the businessman. Who gets popularity? He who is exposed to the public-the politician, the sportsman and the film personality. Who gets veneration? He who is supposed to lead a saintly life, whether genuine or fake. What you do in actual life has a great bearing on what you get in life.

49
CANCER CAN BE CURED

Pat Seed was in her early fifties when she was informed that she had terminal cancer, with only six months to live. Pat Seed could have cursed her fate. Instead, she determined to do something for victims of cancer. She gathered all her energy to do missionary work of raising funds to buy a sophisticated scanner for early detection of cancer. The scanner was to be bought for Christie Hospital in Manchester. She was totally oblivious of anything else, including her own terminal illness. In the process, she was able to outlive her six months (in 1989) pronounced by the doctors. Within a period of six years she raised more than three million pounds for the life-saving equipment. She was presented with an MBE by the Queen of England. She became absolutely free from cancer.

Innumerable patients have been scanned by the equipment bought out of her personal efforts and thereby many lives have been saved.

In a newspaper interview she made the following comment:...

QUESTIONS

1. What is Pat Seed's comment?

2.   What is the implication of this story?

ANSWERS

1.   "I heard about two cancer patients, both men, who like me were given six months to live. One went home, made arrangements for his funeral, and died a fortnight later. The other went home, looked at his seven children and thought: 'How on earth will this lot cope, if I go?' Now twenty years later, those children have grown up and he's still alive."

2.   Mind over matter is the message of this story. Mind is the master and body is the servant. Dr. Carl Simonton of USA has cured hundreds of terminal cancer patients through his meditation techniques which I prefer to call CRVR Meditation. C stands for Conviction that cancer can be cured through Meditation; R refers to Relaxation through Meditation; V implies Visualisation by the patient that the cancerous growth is getting reduced and the last letter R would mean Radiation. This means regular treatment of cancer through radio therapy. Unless such treatment is taken up, it is difficult for the patients to get convinced that cancer can be cured only through meditation. The methodology adopted by Dr. Simonton is highly appreciable. If you are interested to know more about Dr. Carl Simonton's contribution to the medical history of cancer treatment, read the book 'Mind Power' by Nona Coxhead.

50
LOVE YOUR ENEMIES

An English commando killed a German soldier in action in France. He wrote to the dead soldier's mother: "As a soldier. it became my duty to kill your son. I earnestly ask your forgiveness, for I am a Christian. I shall take an opportunity to meet you personally after the war is over."

The dead boy's mother received the note several months later, and replied to the English soldier: "I find it in my heart to forgive you, even though you had killed my son; for I too am a Christian. If we are living after the war is over I hope you will come to Germany to visit me..."

QUESTIONS

1. What could be the concluding clause of her letter to the English Soldier?

2. What is the implication of this story?

Check with our answers only after you have tried to come up with your own.

ANSWERS

1. "That you may take the place of my son in my home, and also in my heart."

2. Forgiveness brings peace of mind, improves relationship and develops sanity.

51
BEWARE OF WHAT YOU THINK MOST OF THE TIME

Mrs. Dwight Morrow's daughter Anne was an outspoken little girl. As we all know, children who talk openly can indeed cause embarrassments.

Once Mrs.Morrow gave a high tea in honour of the senior J. P Morgan. Mrs. Morrow was anxious that when introduced to the great industrialist, Anne might make an unsavoury comment about Morgan's celebrated and conspicuous nose. So she took pains to explain to Anne that making personal observations was impolite. Anne was emphatically cautioned against making any comment upon Morgan's nose, no matter what she might think of it.

When the little girls were brought in for introduction, Mrs. Morrow held her breath as she saw Anne's gaze fix upon Morgan's nose. All went well and the little girls were sent back. With a sigh of relief Mrs. Morrow turned back to her duties as hostess and asked her chief guest,…

QUESTIONS

1. What did she ask?
2. What do we learn out of this story?

Check with our answers only after you have tried to come up with your own.

ANSWERS

1. "And now, Mr. Morgan, will you have cream or lemon in your nose?"

2. Mrs. Morrow's mind was filled with anxiety for possible trouble. Inevitably she invited trouble. Many desire one thing but in their anxiety invite the opposite. They want to become rich but most of the time they are afraid of poverty. Because their minds are filled with thoughts of poverty, the net result is poverty. It is not what you wish that you will get but most of the time what you keep thinking...

52
TIME—DON'T FRITTER AWAY THOUGHTLESSLY

Before dawn, a fisherman went to the river. When reaching the bank he felt something under his foot. It was a small bag of stones. He picked up the bag, put his net aside and squatted on the bank to await the sunrise. In the absence of anything else to do, he lazily picked a stone out of the bag and threw it into the water. Then he cast another stone and then another.

By the time the sun rose he had thrown all the stones away except one. In the dim light, he saw the last stone in his palm. On seeing it he felt very unhappy.

QUESTIONS

1. Why was the fisherman unhappy?

2. What is the implication of this story?

Check with our answers only after you have tried to come up with your own.

ANSWERS

1. He realized that the stone in his palm was a precious stone. He repented that he had been unthinkingly throwing away precious gems.

2. Time is like precious gems that people throw away

thoughtlessly. Many waste their youth and realize it only at the fag end of their lives.

53
DON'T HUMILIATE CHILDREN

As a student, Daniel Webster (author of Webster's Dictionary) was particularly marked for being untidy. Finally the teacher, in exasperation, told him that if he appeared again with such dirty hands she would thrash him. He did appear in the same condition. "Daniel", she said, "hold out your hand." Daniel spat on his palm, with an intention to clean it, rubbed it on his trousers and held it out. The teacher observed all this, in disgust. "Daniel" she said, "if you can find me another hand in this school that is dirtier than yours, I will let you off."

QUESTIONS

1. Did Daniel find another dirtier hand?

2. What is the implication of this story?

Check with our answers only after you have tried to come up with your own.

ANSWERS

1. As soon as the teacher asked Daniel to find out a hand dirtier than the one he showed her, he promptly held out his other hand.

2.   Many eccentric children blossom into geniuses.
The teachers and parents should not underestimate them
or humiliate them.

54
PUNISHMENT HAS VALUE

A blind man was walking down the street with his guide dog. At a street corner while they were waiting for the lights to change, the dog lifted its leg and pissed on the blind man's leg. The blind man did not show any anger but reached into his pocket and took out a dog biscuit. He then bent down as if to give it to the dog.

A bystander who had seen the whole thing went up to the blind man and said, "Sir, it's probably none of my business but I noticed that your dog took undue advantage of your goodness and now you are about to give him a treat. Do you think that is really a good idea?"

The blind man smiled and said,…

QUESTIONS

1. What did the blind say to the bystander?
2. What is the implication of this story?

Check with our answers only after you have tried to come up with your own.

ANSWERS

1. "I am not about to give my dog a treat. I just want to find out where his head is, so I can kick him in the tail."

2.   If the blind man gave the dog a treat for inappropriate behaviour and yelled at the dog when he really wasn't doing anything wrong, the dog would soon become confused and not know what to do.

If you want people to stop doing something wrong, reprimand them adequately. At the same time never hesitate to pay compliments for all the good things they do. Praising and reprimanding should never be done indiscriminately.

55
NOTHING—CARRY IT AROUND

A disciple went to see his Master, informing him that he had come carrying nothing in his hands. The Master told him, "Drop it at once." The disciple repeated, "There is nothing." The Master told him next: "Then carry it around with you."

QUESTIONS

1. Why did the Master ask him to drop nothing?

2. Why did the Master ask him to carry it around?

Check with our answers only after you have tried to come up with your own.

ANSWERS

1. Every disciple comes to the Master with some gift. The disciple in this story came with nothing. The Master asked him to drop it, which means to drop the idea of material possession.

2. When the disciple repeated "It is nothing", which means that he had already dropped the idea of material possession, the Master asked him to carry around the spirit of renunciation. Nothing may also mean the virtue of humility.

56
THE WORD OF WISDOM

A few seekers of truth approached a holy man and begged him to utter a word of wisdom. The word the holy man uttered was,...

QUESTIONS

1. What was the word?

2. What is the implication of this story?

Check with our answers only after you have tried to come up with your own.

ANSWERS

1. "AWARE"

2. Those in quest of spiritual advancement should cultivate the habit of becoming aware of their thoughts, feelings and actions. Most of us in the normal course of life are not aware of our thoughts, feelings, and actions. Our thoughts and feelings are not totally under our control. An angry person is not really aware that he is angry. The moment he is aware of it, his anger will go away. The same is true of all negative emotions. Awareness is the quintessence of all meditation techniques.

57
DON'T CLAIM TO BE 100% ORIGINAL

An orator needlessly used to assert that his speeches were totally original and never borrowed from any other sources.

Once he gave a talk which he thought surpassed any he had given earlier. He expected many in the audience to come and compliment his speech. Since he asserted that his speech was original, no one in the audience was impressed. But only one elderly lady approached him and said, "Your talk was very informative and interesting. I am much impressed, but..."

The orator asked irritably, "Why that 'but'?"

The lady spoke: "But I have seen your speech word by word in a book."

The orator protested emphatically: "Impossible. It is my original speech. Can you show me the book?"

The lady brought the book and showed him.

QUESTIONS

1. Was the orator plagiarizing?
2. What is the implication of this story?

Check with our answers only after you have tried to come up with your own.

ANSWERS

1.   Not really. The elderly lady brought forth a big dictionary. All the words spoken by the orator found a place in that book.

2.   With the advancement of science and technology, the knowledge explosion is so great that no one can claim to be hundred percent original in the modern world.

58
A PROFOUND THOUGHT ON LIFE AND DEATH

A traveller in Africa caught a beautiful multi-hued talking parrot.

Back home in India he fed his pet parrot wonderful seeds and honey, played music for him and generally treated him well.

Two years later, when it was time for the man to return to Africa, he asked his parrot if there was any message he could deliver to the parrot's friends back in the jungle. The parrot told his master to convey his love and say that he was very happy in his cage and enjoying each day.

Back in Africa the traveller delivered the message to the parrots in the jungle. Just as he finished his story, one parrot with tears welling up in his eyes, fell dead. The man was alarmed and concluded that the parrot must have been very close to his pet parrot.

Returning to India, he told his pet what had happened. As he finished his story, the pet parrot's eyes welled up with tears and he fell dead in his cage. The man was astounded, but figured that his pet died from the despair of hearing of the death of his close friend back in the jungle. He opened up the cage and tossed the dead bird into the trash heap. Immediately his pet parrot flew up to a tree.

The trader said to him, "So you are not dead after all, why did you do that?"

The parrot answered, "Because that bird back in Africa sent me a very important message."

"What was the message?" the trader inquired impatiently.

QUESTIONS

1.   What was the message given by the bird?

2.   What is the implication of this story?

Check with our answers only after you have tried to come up with your own.

ANSWERS

1.   "He told me if you want to escape from your cage, you must die while you are alive."

2.   This statement has profound meaning. If you want to be totally free from all sufferings in this world "you should be dead while you are alive." The word 'dead' can be interpreted in many ways. When you develop dispassionate attitude to life, you are practically 'dead'. If you cultivate the virtue of renunciation, you can be considered as 'dead'. If you are humble, you are 'dead' to your egoistic tendency. We suffer a lot on this planet only because of our egoistic tendency. If you are able to

lead a life free from desire, you can be considered as totally free from the cage of the desire for wealth, name, fame and other pleasures of life. The state of consciousness of 'being dead while alive' is known in yogic parlance as 'Samadhi.' Yogis explain this state of consciousness as the heightened form of bliss and ecstasy. It is not a stage to be reached at a particular point of time but a way of life to be led with dispassionate attitude. To reach this state of consciousness requires constant awareness of our own thoughts, feelings and actions. To attain this state, one need not renounce the world, go to Himalayas and do meditation. Anyone can reach this state just by changing his attitude to life.

59
GET INTOXICATED NATURALLY

George Russell, the Irish poet was a teetotaller. Whenever he was offered a drink he would politely decline by saying,...

QUESTIONS

1. How did George Russell avoid social drinking?

2. What is the implication of this story?

Check with our answers only after you have tried to come up with your own.

ANSWERS

1. His usual answer was, "No thank you. You see, I was born intoxicated!"

2. Social drinking can become the thin end of the wedge towards alcoholism. If one is firm and consistent in not drinking liquor, under any circumstances, people would in due course, hold him in high esteem. People who are afraid of public opinion will never stand out in the crowd.

60
THE COURAGE OF A HANDICAPPED WOMAN

Hilary started life just like any other child, healthy and strong. She grew up to be very good at games and dancing. She became a dance teacher. Then suddenly a terrible disease struck. Hilary could feel and hear everything, but she could not move. She could not move her mouth or her eyelids. She couldn't sing; she couldn't talk; she couldn't make a sound. Because she could not chew or eat, she was fed through tubes and kept alive with a breathing machine. The only thing she could move was the big toe of her right foot. Her big toe would give a tiny flicker, 1/16th of an inch, less than 2mm, when she wanted it to. The only other thing Hilary could do was to hear.

But Hilary didn't just give up and die. For ten years, she carried on speaking and smiling, praying and helping through her big toe. At first she had to spell the words out, but after three years, scientific invention came to her rescue. Hilary got a Possum machine. With its help, she was able to operate a whole range of switches, turn on the radio and most importantly, operate a typewriter. Letters poured from her; she wrote poems and articles. She worked so hard for handicapped people that in 1973 The Queen of England wrote to tell her that she had been awarded the MBE for her brave work...

QUESTION

What do you learn from Hilary's story?

Check with our answers only after you have tried to come up with your own.

ANSWER

With our entire limbs intact, do we not, on many occasions, feel depressed over minor things?

61
BE A ROLE MODEL TO YOUR CHILDREN

Five-year-old Deepak used to sleep alone in his room. One day his father was with him at bedtime. Deepak wanted his father to tell him some stories, which he did.

After quite some time Deepak felt sleepy and told his father, "Now, Daddy, I have to say my prayers." He knelt down beside his bed, joined his hands, raised his eyes to heaven and prayed, "Now I lay down to sleep, I pray the Lord my soul to keep; if I should die before I wake up, I pray the Lord my soul to take." This was his usual prayer, but that night he looked up at his Dad, then raised his eyes to heaven and prayed aloud, "Dear God, make me a great big good man, like my Daddy. Thank you God." In a moment he was in bed and in five minutes he slept.

And then the father knelt by his son's bedside and prayed.

QUESTIONS

1. What was the father's prayer?
2. What is the implication of this story?

Check with our answers only after you have tried to come up with your own.

ANSWERS

1.   "Dear Lord, make me a great big good man like my boy thinks I am."

2.   Every child holds a very high opinion about its parents. It is left to the parents to live up to that opinion. The best gift that parents can offer to their children is their own life's example. Parents should be role models to their children.

62
RETURN GOOD FOR EVIL

A rich old man divided his property among his three sons, all except a costly diamond ring. To decide who was to inherit the ring, he asked them to travel for a while and return on a certain day. He who would have done the noblest deed during that time would receive the diamond ring.

The sons did as they were told. After their return, each described what he had done. The eldest son said that a man gave him all his wealth without any bond. He might have kept it all for himself, but he returned it to the man, every rupee with interest added. The father said that he had acted well, but this was expected of him.

The second son described how he had saved a child's life from the roaring sea, risking his own life. The father commended his brave deed but said that to deserve the diamond ring, the act had to be nobler.

The father gave the diamond ring to the youngest son.

QUESTIONS

1. What was the youngest son's deed that deserved the diamond ring?

2.   What is the implication of this story?

Check with our answers only after you have tried to come up with your own.

ANSWERS

1.   The youngest son said that when he was tending sheep, he saw his bitter enemy sleeping on the brink of a precipice; he could have fallen to his death. But the son of the rich man woke him up and thus saved him from death.

The father said with pride and joy that his youngest son kept no hatred for his enemy and acted like a true gentleman. He gave him his ring as a reward for the noblest deed.

2.   The first son displayed the virtue of honesty. Many people are honest. There is nothing special about it. The second son risked his life. At the spur of the moment, many people risk their lives to save someone in danger. This could be considered as an instinctual behaviour. The third son saved the life of his enemy. Unless there is absence of hatred, this is not possible. Removing hatred from one's consciousness, and developing love for his enemy could be considered as the noblest of all deeds. It requires many years of conscious effort to develop this virtue.

63
BE WITH THE PRESENT

On the music maestro Arturo Toscanini's eightieth birthday, someone asked his son, Walter, what his father ranked as his most important achievement.

QUESTIONS

1. What was Walter's answer?

2. What is the implication of this story?

Check with our answers only after you have tried to come up with your own.

ANSWERS

1. The son replied, "For him there can be no such thing. Whatever he happens to be doing at that moment is the most important thing in his life-whether it is conducting a symphony or peeling an orange."

2. Be with the present. Consider every moment of your life as glorious as possible. The only reality is the present moment. The past is dead and the future is yet to be born.

64
REPENTANCE—A VIRTUE TO BE DEVELOPED

One day Frederick William I visited a prison at Postman and listened to a number of pleas for pardon from the prisoners who had grievances against the injustices done to them by law. All said they had suffered imprisonment on account of prejudiced judges, prejudiced witnesses, and unscrupulous lawyers. From cell to cell the tales of wronged innocence continued, until the King stopped at the door of one cell inhabited by a surly inmate who said nothing. Surprised at his silence Frederick said jocularly, "Well I suppose you are innocent too."

"No, your Majesty", was the startling response; "I am guilty and richly deserve all that I get."

On hearing this, the King shouted at the jail authorities and asked them to do something urgently.

QUESTIONS

1. What did the King ask the jail authorities to do?

2. What is the implication of this story?

Check with our answers only after you have tried to come up with your won.

ANSWERS

1. The King called the jail authorities and ordered them: "Come and get rid of this rascal quickly, before he corrupts this fine lot of innocent people that you are holding."

2. The prisoner who admitted his guilt showed certain potential for improvement. The others were not likely to change.

65
DEATH—THE GREAT EQUALIZER

An old man was very hungry. There was nothing in the house to eat. So he stole a rooster from a chicken farm.

The rooster was boiling in the pot when someone knocked at the door. The old man thought it was the owner of the bird and did not open the door. But the knocking continued and he could not ignore it. "Who are you and what do you want?" he asked the man standing at the door.

"I am God and I want something to eat."

"I am sorry but I cannot give you anything" said the old man.

"Why?" asked the Lord. "I smell food and so I know you can share something with me."

"That may be, but I would not like to feed someone who does not treat everyone alike. I notice that to some you give much; to others little."

"Yes, that is true", said the visitor, and departed.

Soon there came another knock at the door. A woman stood there this time. "And who are you?" asked the man.

"I am the Virgin Mary", said the woman, "and I would like something to eat."

"I am sorry", said the man "but I cannot share my food with you."

"Why?" asked the Virgin.

"Because" said the man, "you are one of those who does not treat everyone alike. To some you give much; to others little." The Virgin had nothing to say and so she left.

And now the rooster was cooked and the man was ready to sit down and eat. Another knock was heard. "I wonder who can be this time?" said the man. At the door stood Death, and said, "I smelled your rooster. I came here to share the food with you.

QUESTIONS

1. What was the man's answer?
2. What is the implication of this story?

Check with our answers only after you have tried to come up with your own.

ANSWERS

1. The old man reacted positively to Death. He invited Death inside, saying, "Aren't you the one who treats everyone alike?"

"That is so", said Death. "I have no favourites. The

poor, the rich, the young, the old, the sick, all look alike to me."

"That is why you may come in and share my food" said the man. Death entered and the two had a grand feast.

2.   While death has often been viewed as an enemy by those in good circumstances, it is a "Great Equalizer".

66
HANDICAP IS NO BARRIER TO ACHIEVEMENTS

Henri Vicardi was born in 1912 in New York, to immigrant parents. He was born without normal legs. He spent most of his early life in a hospital. Until he was twenty-seven, he did not receive his artificial legs.

But what a life he had lived!

He became one of the most respected figures in the fields of rehabilitation and education. He had devoted his life to ensuring that severely disabled individuals might have all the opportunities to achieve to their fullest potential.

In 1952 he established the internationally famous Human Resources Center in Elberton, Long Island. He had demonstrated to the world that the disabled can fully integrate with every phase of life.

Henri has been an advisor to every President from Franklin Roosevelt to Ronald Reagan. His honours and rewards are many. He is highly respected and admired across the country and is well known for his positive attitude and his endearing sense of humour.

Once an interviewer asked him, "Henri, from where did you get such a positive attitude toward life?" His answer was a classic. He said,...

QUESTIONS

1. What was Henri Vicardi's answer?

2. What is the implication of this story?

Check with our answers only after you have tried to come up with your own.

ANSWERS

1. "When the turn came for another crippled boy or girl to be sent to the world, God consulted his council of Ministers and they suggested that they could be sent to the Vicardi family."

2. Handicap is no barrier to achievements. If you produce results you are acceptable to the society.

67
AWARE OF YOUR NEGATIVE EMOTIONS

A young learned man made a long journey to see a celebrated sage living in a remote village. He was very much vexed with the difficult journey. When he finally arrived at his destination, he angrily undid his shoelaces, tossed his shoes into a corner and pushed the door open with a heavy thud. Then he went in, and offered his respects to the wise man. The wise man, who had observed his impatient behaviour, refused to accept his homage and asked him to do something.

QUESTIONS

1. What did the wise man ask the traveller to do?

2. What is the implication of this story?

Check with our answers only after you have tried to come up with your own.

ANSWERS

1. "First go and offer your apologies to the shoes and the door."

2. Anger shown on inanimate objects reflects a bad temperament. It is not conducive to health and happiness. Offering apologies to inanimate objects may look

ridiculous, but it will remind the person to become aware of his negative emotions.

68
THE FIRST STEP TO ENLIGHTENMENT

The guru promised a scholar a revelation of greater consequence than anything contained in the scriptures.

The scholar was eager to know. The guru said, "Go out in the rain and raise your head and arms heavenward. That will bring you the first revelation."

The next day the scholar came to report: "I followed your advice and water flowed down my neck and I felt like a perfect fool."

"Well, said the guru...

QUESTIONS

1.   What did the guru say to the scholar?

2.   What is the implication of this story?

Check with our answers only after you have tried to come up with your own.

ANSWERS

1.   "Well, for the first day that's quite a revelation, isn't it?"

2.   Feeling like a perfect fool is the first step towards enlightenment. Wisdom comes from realizing one's

inability to understand the mysteries and intricacies of the creation of this universe and its operational facets.

69
DEVELOP CREATIVE THINKING

When an assistant in the public library told the librarian that certain books were never read because the subject-matter was too difficult, the librarian thought for a moment and devised a method which ensured that every book on the shelf went into immediate circulation.

QUESTIONS

1. What was the method adopted by the librarian?

2. What is the implication of this story?

Check with our answers only after you have tried to come up with your own.

ANSWERS

1. The librarian brought all those books which were not circulated, put them in an attractive display window with a sign.

Warning: These books are difficult to read and require advanced understanding capabilities.

2. A little time spent in creative thinking can bring new solutions to problems. Everyone is endowed with creativity but only a few use this ability. This story brings out the librarian's creative ability.

70
FRIENDS—MAKE A CAREFUL SELECTION

A monkey was the king's pet. The king kept it in his own room. Once when he went to bed, the monkey was asked to keep a watch and protect the sleeping king. While doing the security assignment, the monkey saw a fly coming and sitting on the king's nose. He drove it away but again it came and rested at the same place. The monkey lost its temper and taking its sword struck at the fly; with what disastrous result, can you guess?

QUESTIONS

1. Did the monkey kill the fly?

2. What is the implication of this story?

Check with our answers only after you have tried to come up with your own.

ANSWERS

1. The fortunate fly flew away humming and unfortunately the king lost the tip of his nose. Thank God! He could save his head.

2. It is dangerous to make friends with unwise people though they may be very sincere, because such friends may innocently put us into trouble.

71
HONESTY—PAYS YOU IN THE LONG RUN

A soldier had done some business transaction with the natives at Aden. The natives, being ignorant of the value of English coins, sent too much money. The soldier faithfully returned the surplus money. His friend said, "Don't be a silly fool. Why return the money when the natives don't know the correct value of English coins?" The solider replied.

QUESTIONS

1. What was the soldier's reply?

2. What is the implication of this story?

Check with our answers only after you have tried to come up with your own.

ANSWERS

1. "I am not going to sell my character for a few coppers."

2. Honesty and sincerity will pay in the long run, though in the short run it may cause some losses. A person's credibility can be established through honest acts in certain trying situations.

72
PREACH ONLY WHAT YOU PRACTISE

A little girl was extra fond of sweets. Her mother's efforts to control her liking were not having any effect. As a last resort, the mother took her to Gandhiji for advice.

Gandhiji asked them to come after three weeks. When they went next, Gandhiji advised the girl not to eat too much sweets and explained how it could be harmful to health. At this juncture the mother asked him, "You could have given this advice at our earlier visit itself. Why did you prefer to postpone it for three weeks?" Gandhiji replied,…

QUESTIONS

1. What was Gandhiji's reply?

2. What is the implication of this story?

Check with our answers only after you have tried to come up with your own.

ANSWERS

1. "Three weeks ago I myself was addicted to eating sweet foods."

2. During the three weeks period Gandhiji restrained from taking sweet foods. Once he was able to control his desire for sweet foods, he could give advice to others. Any advice carries weight only if the person giving the advice practises it.

73
THE EFFICACY OF MEDITATION

A wood-carver called Ching had just finished work on a bell-frame. Everyone who saw it marvelled for it seemed to be the work of spirits. When the Duke of Lu saw it, he asked, "What sort of genius is yours that you could make such a thing?"

The wood-carver replied: "Sir, I am only a simple workman. I am no genius. But there is one thing. When I am going to make a bell-frame I meditate to calm my mind. When I have meditated for three days I think no more about rewards or emoluments. When I have meditated for five days, I no longer think of praise or blame, skillfulness or awkwardness. When I have meditated for seven days I suddenly forget my limbs, my body; no, I forget my very self. I lose consciousness of the court and my surroundings. Only my skill remains. In that state I walk into the forest and examine each tree until I find one in which I see the bell-frame in all its perfection. Then my hands go to the task. "He further continued,...

QUESTIONS

1. What did the wood-carver further say to the nobleman?

2.   What is the implication of this story?

ANSWERS

1.   "Having set my self aside, nature meets nature in the work that is performed through me. This no doubt is the reason why everyone says that the finished product is the work of spirits."

2.   Ching is a model Karma Yogi. When one is totally involved in what one is doing without bothering about name, fame, money or position, one is capable of producing marvellous work.

74
GRAB EVERY OPPORTUNITY TO HELP

Dr. Adolph Lorenz of Vienna had become very famous for bloodless surgery. He had cured a wealthy merchant's daughter through his new device. He made a trip to the United States to explain his techniques to the medical fraternity.

In New York, the doctor was put up in a posh hotel. He was much protected by guards. One afternoon, craving for a little solitude, he slipped out of the hotel for a stroll. Without warning, a thunderstorm began raging and the good doctor was caught in a downpour. Seeking shelter, he rang the doorbell of a house close by. But when he asked the woman who had opened the door whether he could come inside, she angrily cried out. "There is trouble enough in this house. You may go somewhere else", and slammed the door. Dr. Lorenz, totally drenched, stood outside until a car came with guards and took him back to the hotel.

The next day there was a big write-up about Dr. Lorenz as a great healer, with his photo on the front page of the newspaper. The inhospitable lady recognized that the person to whom she refused entry into her house was the very same Dr. Lorenz. The woman's daughter suffered from the same illness which the doctor had treated in

Vienna and the lady had written a letter to the hotel, entreating Dr. Lorenz to come to her house to treat her daughter. Unfortunately, she shut the door in his face when God had brought him there.

QUESTION

What is the implication of this story?

Check with our answer only after you have tried to come up with your own.

ANSWER

Everyday we are presented with a variety of occasions to help others. Do we grab such opportunities? At every doorstep opportunity waits for us to serve our fellow-men.

75
SEE THE POSITIVE SIDE OF EVERYTHING

Babu informed his mother that he had given his name for any part in his school drama. His mother was anxious that he should obtain one of the main roles.

On the day of the selection, she asked him, after school hours were over, whether he had been selected. Babu told her excitedly,...

QUESTIONS

1. What did Babu tell his mother?

2. What is the implication of this story?

Check with our answers only after you have tried to come up with your own.

ANSWERS

1. "I've been chosen to clap and cheer."

2. When you are disappointed with your lot in life remember Babu's story. Learn to see the positive side of anything.

76
DEVELOP POSITIVE ATTITUDE TO LIFE

Donald B. Macmillan, the Arctic explorer, received a letter from an unknown person, when setting out on an expedition to the Far North. Inscribed on the cover were the words: "To be opened when everything has gone dead wrong."

QUESTIONS

1.   When do you think Macmillan opened the letter?

2.   What is the implication of this story?

Check with our answers only after you have tried to come up with your own.

ANSWERS

1.   The letter was not opened even after fifty years. Macmillan informed his friends that during all the time nothing had gone dead wrong in his life.

2.   Whether you think that everything is wrong or good in life is just an attitude. Choosing to develop a positive attitude towards life leads to happiness.

77
BE NATURAL AND REALISTIC

A transport company had advertised for the post of assistants. At the job interview the applicants were asked to move a very heavy safe from one place to another. The job applicants struggled to move the safe, thinking that was a test of their brawn, but in vain. Then came Johnny, a well-built muscular man. When he was asked to move the safe, he said....

QUESTIONS

1. What did the applicant say to the interviewers?

2. What is the implication of this story?

ANSWERS

1. "Are you kidding" I can't move that safe by myself. I need help. "He got the job.

2. Many fail in an interview because they make lot of assumptions of the expectations of the interviewers and try to answer or do accordingly. To be successful, one should be natural, abiding by the dictates of one's genius. We may go wrong when we make assumptions.

78
BUILD YOUR MANSION IN HEAVEN

A wealthy lady became inordinately proud of her fine mansion and landscaped garden. She was an avowed materialist. Her faithful old gardener looked at everything differently. Despite his poverty, he saw the world as a wonderful place, full of beautiful simple things—the flowers he tended, the birds who serenaded him at work and the delicacy of scudding clouds. From his meagre income, he was always ready to help where he could.

The lady died, and as she looked around heaven for her rightful abode she was directed to a mean, tumble-down shack. "I think you have made a mistake" she said, "I have always been used to something really worthy. I had a charming house—sixteen luxurious rooms—the best that money could buy."

Then spotting a delightful dwelling close by, nearing completion, she brightened. "Ah, now, what about that one? That's the sort of place I'd like."

"Sorry Madam, you can't have that; we are getting that ready for your gardener when he comes."

"My gardener? But he's used to a tiny cottage; why couldn't you prepare one like that for me?"

And the celestial housing officer replied;...

QUESTIONS

1. What was the celestial officer's reply?

2. What is the implication of this story?

Check with our answers only after you have tried to come up with your own.

ANSWERS

1. "Impossible, Madam. It's right out of our hands; we can only build with the materials sent up by the future occupants. He's sent us magnificent material, always. Yours was a bit substandard, you must admit."

2. It is not the material possessions but right attitudes to life that matter a lot for success and happiness.

79
SHOWER UNCONDITIONAL LOVE TO YOUR CHILDREN

As a single parent with a teenage son, a lady had gone through many financial difficulties. They lived in an old mobile home with all sorts of structural problems. When one of her son's friends, who lived in a beautiful house, ran away for a few days, the woman was puzzled.

"Why did he do it?" she asked, "he had everything he could possibly wish for."

"Well, Mum, it's like this", her son said...

QUESTIONS

1. What did he say?

2. What is the implication of this story?

Check with our answers only after you have tried to come up with your own.

ANSWERS

1. "Jimmy has a lot of environment, but not much love, and I have a lot of love but not much environment."

2. Love of parents has immeasurable contribution to the growth of children. Unconditional love should be showered on them.

80
CONQUER THE FEAR OF DEATH

Friends advised Julius Caesar to be more cautious about his safety. "Better not walk among the people without arms" they said, "Also, there would be someone to protect you all the time."

Caesar replied,...

QUESTIONS

1. What was Caesar's reply?

2. What do you learn from this story?

Check with our answers only after you have tried to come up with your own.

ANSWERS

1. He who lives in fear of death, every moment feels its torture: I will die but once."

2. Unless we conquer the fear of death, we won't be able to achieve anything.

81
LEARN TO APPRECIATE WHAT YOU HAVE

Women in some parts of Mexico are fortunate. In these parts hot springs and cold springs cascade side by side. The women often wash their clothes in the hot springs and rinse them in the cold springs.

A tourist, who had watched this natural phenomenon, was fascinated. He remarked to his Mexican friend, "I guess the women think of old Mother Nature as pretty generous." To which his friend replied,...

QUESTIONS

1. What was the Mexican's reply?
2. What is the implication of this story?

Check with our answers only after you have tried to come up with your own.

ANSWERS

1. "No, Sir. There is much grumbling because Mother Nature supplies no soap."

2. We never appreciate what we have but only complain of what we lack.

82
RENDER SIMPLE ACTS OF KINDNESS TO SOCIETY

A king had a heavy boulder placed on the road and asked a minister to hide and watch to find who would remove it. Men of various classes came and worked their way round it, some loudly blaming the king for not keeping the highway clear, but all dodging the duty by getting it out of the way. At last a poor peasant came to town carrying his burden of vegetables for sale. He saw the boulder, laid down his load, and rolled the stone into the gutter.

QUESTIONS

1. How did the king reward him for his act of kindness?

2. What is the implication of this story?

Check with our answers only after you have tried to come up with your own.

ANSWERS

1. After removing the boulder the peasant noticed a purse right under it. He opened the purse and found it full of gold pieces with a note from the king saying it was for the one who would remove the boulder.

2.   We have civic duties to our society. In our mad pursuit to acquire wealth, name and fame, we forget to render simple acts of kindness to society at large. With a little more civic sense, society would progress better.

83
THE HAPPY MAN

A king was dying. All the doctors in the kingdom could not cure him. Finally, a holy man was brought.

The king said, "Holy Sire, I am not ready to die yet. I depend on your wisdom and holiness to help me live long. Can you help me?"

The holy man said, "That is easy. You just have to wear a shirt belonging to the happiest man in the kingdom. The cure is certain if you make sure to find out that person."

The king ordered his servants, "Do as the holy man says. Go and get me a shirt belonging to the happiest person in the kingdom."

They went out in their search. With great difficulty they could find that person in a remote village. There was no doubt that he was the happiest person in the kingdom, but unfortunately they could not fulfill the instruction of the holy man.

QUESTIONS

1. Why?
2. What is the implication of this story?

Check with our answers only after you have tried to come up with your own.

ANSWERS

1.   The happiest man in the kingdom did not have a shirt.

2.   Material possessions alone do not bring happiness. The more you accumulate, the greater would be the problem.

84
THE VALUE OF MEDITATION

Lord Buddha had a disciple who had been a devotee for many years. One day the Buddha asked him, "Monk, what is your age?" The monk replied, "Five", The Buddha was surprised, "Five? You look at least seventy. What kind of answer is this?" The monk replied,...

QUESTIONS

1. What was the monk's reply?

2. What is the implication of this story?

Check with our answers only after you have tried to come up with your own.

ANSWERS

1. "I started meditating only five years ago. I have realized my worthiness only after beginning meditation. Hence I am only five."

2. The reality of life is unveiled through meditation. Only those who meditate regularly can experience its enchantment. It cannot be described in words.

85
A UNIQUE
PUNISHMENT

Rustom was a brave and big-hearted man. He was commander-in-chief of the army of King Chosroes of Persia.

Idolized by his soldiers, Rustom took it into his head to plan a revolution. Word of it got to the king, who called a council of ministers.

All the ministers agreed that the traitor should be put in chains and tried.

The king thought over the matter the whole night and in the morning sent for his army leader. Instead of putting him under arrest, the king bestowed upon his General new favours and marks of esteem. Rustom repented and resolved to be more loyal for the rest of his life.

Seeing the traitor march from the palace a free man, the king's ministers complained, "Your Majesty, why don't you put him in chains?"

The king replied, "Of course I have put him in chains. But those chains are invisible and you can't see them..."

The ministers were baffled at the king's answer.

QUESTIONS

1. What was the kind of chain the king put on his

General?

2. What is the implication of this story?

Check with our answers only after you have tried to come up with your own.

ANSWERS

1. "I have put his heart in chains."

2. Love wins better than punishment.

86
A BITTER TRUTH FOR PARENTS

A mother was shocked to hear her son tell a lie. Taking the youngster aside for a heart-to-heart talk, she graphically explained what happens to liars.

"A tall black man with red fiery eyes and two sharp horns grabs little boys who tell lies and carries them off at night. He takes them to Mars where they have to work in a dark canyon for 50 years! Now", she concluded, "you won't tell a lie again, will you, dear?"

"No, Mum", replied the son, gravely. "But...

QUESTIONS

1. What did the boy intend to say further?

2. What is the implication of this story?

Check with our answers only after you have tried to come up with your own.

ANSWERS

1. "But you tell better lies, Mum."

2. Children learn to tell lies from the elders. With them it does not work to say. "Do as I tell and not as I do."

87
LOOK WITHIN

A man was frantically searching for his lost key under a lamp post. A passerby asked him, "Where did you drop your key?"

The man answered, "Inside the house."

"Then why are you searching under this lamp post?" asked the passerby.

QUESTIONS

1. What was the man's reply?

2. What is the implication of this story?

Check with our answers only after you have tried to come up with your own.

ANSWERS

1. "Because there is light here," answered the man.

2. That is what we do every time we look outside of ourselves for solutions to problems.

88
SOCRATES CHOICE OF DISCIPLES

Socrates was once asked by his disciple, "Why is it, Sir, that you tell everybody who wants to become your disciple to look into this pond here and tell you what he sees?"

Socrates answered,...

QUESTIONS

1. What was Socrates' answer?

2. What is the implication of this story?

Check with our answers only after you have tried to come up with your own.

ANSWERS

1. "That is very simple. I am ready to accept all those who tell me they see the fish swimming around. But those who see only their own image mirrored in the water are in love with their ego. I have no use for them."

2. Have interests outside of yourself.

89
PAY THE PRICE

A man came to buy a saddle for his horse. He saw a fine piece and asked, "How much?"

"Five hundred rupees", the shop-owner said.

"But that is too much", the man replied. As it is, the saddle is overly decorated. Remove some of the decoration and cut down the price."

"All right", the shop-owner said and took away some of the decoration. He said "Now, it will be Rs. 400."

"Rs. 400? Even that is too much. There is still some decoration you can remove."

So it went on till the price was brought down to Rs. 250. Even so, the customer found the price too much.

At last the shop-owner said. "All right, sir. The saddle will cost you nothing."

The buyer asked excitedly, "Nothing? Wonderful. What do I get?"

The shop-owner told him,…

QUESTIONS

1. What did the shop-owner tell him?
2. What is the implication of this story?

Check with our answers only after you have tried to come up with your own.

ANSWERS

1. "Nothing."

2. We get according to our willingness to pay. This holds well in the spiritual realm too.

90
QUINTESSENCE OF SELF-IMPROVEMENT

"You should build a better world", God said.

I questioned: "How?"

"The world is such a wondrous place.

So complicated now"

"I so small and useless am;

There's nothing I can do!"

But God, the all-wise and kind, replied:...

QUESTIONS

1. What was God's reply?

2. What is the implication of this story?

Check with our answers only after you have tried to come up with your own.

ANSWERS

1. "JUST BUILD A BETTER YOU."

2. This is the quintessence of self-improvement. All programmes relating to personality development aim at building a better person.

91
LINCOLN'S COMPASSION

A telegram from one of his Generals was on Lincoln's desk while an old man was pleading pardon for his son. Lincoln turned to him gently but firmly. "I am sorry. I can do nothing for you", he said with finality. "Listen to this telegram I received from General Butler yesterday. President Lincoln, I pray you not to interfere with the court-martial of the army. You will destroy all discipline among our soldiers."

Then greatly affected by the hopeless despair on the old man's face, Lincoln said, "By jingo! Butler or no Butler, here goes!"

The old man read, "Job Smith not to be shot until further orders from me—Abraham Lincoln".

He expressed disappointment. "Why, I thought it was a pardon! You may order him shot next week."

"My old friend the President replied,...

QUESTIONS

1. What was Abraham Lincoln's reply?
2. What is the implication of this story?

Check with our answers only after you have tried to come up with your own.

ANSWERS

1. "I see you are not very well acquainted with me. Your son will never die till orders come from me to shoot him; he will live to be a great deal older than Methuselah."

2. Lincoln's kindness, in going out of the way to help people, was one of the reasons he is considered as a humanitarian par excellence.

92
THE COST OF BEING HONEST

A man was very grateful when a taxi driver called to tell him that he had left his wallet on the back seat. He offered to reward the driver but he said, "If you don't mind, just let me know how much there is in your purse."

When he informed him, the driver wrote the amount in a notebook and explained,...

QUESTIONS

1. What was the taxi driver's explanation?

2. What is the implication of this story?

Check with our answers only after you have tried to come up with your own.

ANSWERS

1. "I'm keeping track of what it's costing me to be honest."

2. The peace of mind that honesty provides is immeasurable.

93
LIFE IS A SERIES OF CHOICES

Brahma, the Lord of Creation, wanted to play a trick on human beings. Everyone's ultimate objective is to be happy but, by and large, no one is quite happy. Therefore, Brahma decided to hide happiness, so that he should find happiness if he searched for it.

A council was held to advise Brahma.

Brahma informed the council of the agenda: "I want to play a trick on man. Everyone is hunting for happiness and we should hide it in such a way that they should seldom find it."

Some suggested, "Bury it deep in the earth."

But Brahma said, "No, man will dig deep into the earth and find it."

"Well, shall we sink happiness into the deepest ocean?"

But again Brahma replied, "No, he will eventually explore the depths of every ocean and will surely some day find and take it."

The council concluded, "Then it seems there is no place on earth or in the sea that man will not reach."

Then Brahma said,...

QUESTIONS

1. What did Brahma say?

2. What is the implication of this story?

Check with our answers only after you have tried to come up with your own.

ANSWERS

1. "Here is what we will do with man's happiness" said Brahma. "We will hide it deep down in man himself, for he will never think of looking for it there."

2. Life is a series of choices. If you are happy, that is your choice. If you are miserable, that also is your choice. Happiness is within our reach. The moment we realize this simple truth, we will become transformed persons.

94
PUBLIC SPEECH—HOW SHOULD IT BE

At a banquet, a speaker was holding forth on a subject which held very little interest for most of the audience. Unable to stand it any longer, one of them slipped quietly out. Just outside the door he bumped into another sufferer who had gone out much earlier.

"Has he finished yet?" he was asked.

The man who had just escaped replied,...

QUESTIONS

1. What was his reply?

2. What is the implication of this story?

ANSWERS

1. "Yes, long ago, but he doesn't stop."

2. A public talk should be to the point and sparkling.

95
IRRESISTIBLE DESIRE TO LIVE

The court jester kept the king in good humour with his quips, and entertained the royal household.

On one occasion, the king was displeased with a retort of the jester and condemned him to death. But after a while the king realized the rashness of his decree. It was however supposed to be legally impossible for the king to change any sentence he set on a subject. So he asked the jester: "In consideration of your faithful services, I will permit you to select the manner in which you prefer to die. "The jester instantly answered,...

QUESTIONS

1. What was the jester's answer?

2. What is the implication of this story?

Check with our answers only after you have tried to come up with your own.

ANSWERS

1. "I select to die of old age."

2. With presence of mind, one can manage any situation in life.

96
DO SOMETHING JUST FOR FUN

Uncle Bill was well known for his prodigious strength. One day a circus man came to challenge him. He rode his horse up inside Uncle Bill's gate. He closed the gate and said, "I heard about you back in town. Now I want to see who the better man is."

Uncle Bill did not say a word. His big hands whipped out, grabbed the strong circus man, and hurled him over the gate. He brushed himself off and in a gentle way asked the circus man. "Anything else you want?"

"Yes", said the stunned circus performer...

QUESTIONS

1. What did the circus man want from Uncle Bill?
2. What is the implication of this story?

Check with our answer only after you have tried to come up with your own.

ANSWERS

1. "Would you please throw me my horse too!"
2. This story is told in a humorous vein. Life must have scope for actions that are done just for fun. Every single thing does not need to have philosophical significance.

97
THE REMEDY FOR DEPRESSION

A businessman became depressed and nervous. The psychiatrist, whom he consulted, questioned him carefully and told him, "For starters, I will give you one exercise. Go to the railway station and look for someone to help."

As ordered, the businessman went to the station and looked around. He saw an old woman crying in a corner of a waiting room. She had come to Bangalore to visit her daughter, but has lost the address and did not have enough money to go to a hotel. The businessman found the daughter's address in the telephone directory, and took the old lady there in a taxi. On the way, he gave her pleasant surprise by buying her some roses. Her joy was patent.

As soon as the man was free he rushed to telephone the psychiatrist and informed him,...

QUESTIONS

1. What did the businessman inform the psychiatrist?

2. What is the implication of this story?

Check with our answers only after you have tried to come up with your own.

ANSWERS

1.   "Now I realize the true joy in life."

2.   True joy comes when we render service to the needy without having even an iota of expectation.

98
DEVELOP PRESENCE OF MIND

A teacher of psychology, F. L. Thomson of San Francisco, was accosted by a hold-up man late one night. Thinking quickly, Thomson asked the thief for a dime and started a rambling hard-luck story. Astonished, the bandit admitted his original intention and gave his intended victim a ten-cent piece. The professor went home with his dime and the $200 that was in his wallet.

QUESTION

What is the implication of this story?

Check with our answer only after you have tried to come up with your own.

ANSWER

Presence of mind saves many a situation.

99
DISCARD HERO WORSHIP

There was once a famous magician who astounded everyone by making almost any object disappear. His showmanship attracted many followers who attended every performance. One day he performed before an audience on board a ship. The ship sank in a sudden storm, but the magician and his admirers managed to make it to a lifeboat.

"Wonderful" the people praised and applauded the magician. They further asked him,...

QUESTIONS

1.   What did they ask the magician?
2.   What is the implication of this story?

Check with our answers only after you have tried to come up with your own.

ANSWERS

1.   "But tell us, where did you hide the ship?" They truly believed the disappearance of the ship was another magic feat of his.

2.   Hero-worship is born out of gullibility. People idolize some persons who have specialized knowledge which may seem to be astounding to the common run of people.

100
THE LOVE OF GOD

There was a neurotic person who was always tense, anxious, irritated, depressed and selfish. Every one of his friends and relatives insisted that he must change. The man himself made earnest attempts to change for the better, but nothing happened. He remained the same. The more they insisted, the more he felt powerless and trapped.

One day one of his closest friends said, "Don't change. Don't change. I love you as you are."

Those words were music to his ears, "Don't change. Don't change. Don't change... I love you as you are."

He relaxed and felt comfortable. As there were no more compulsions to change, he suddenly changed!

QUESTION

What is the implication of this story?

Check with our answer only after you have tried to come up with your own.

ANSWER

He could not really change till he found someone to love him whether he changed or not. This is the way God loves every one of us?

JAICO PUBLISHING HOUSE
Elevate Your Life. Transform Your World.

ESTABLISHED IN 1946, Jaico Publishing House is home to world-transforming authors such as Sri Sri Paramahansa Yogananda, Osho, the Dalai Lama, Sri Sri Ravi Shankar, Sadhguru, Robin Sharma, Deepak Chopra, Jack Canfield, Eknath Easwaran, Devdutt Pattanaik, Khushwant Singh, John Maxwell, Brian Tracy, and Stephen Hawking.

Our late founder Mr. Jaman Shah first established Jaico as a book distribution company. Sensing that independence was around the corner, he aptly named his company Jaico ('Jai' means victory in Hindi). In order to service the significant demand for affordable books in a developing nation, Mr. Shah initiated Jaico's own publications. Jaico was India's first publisher of paperback books in the English language.

While self-help, religion and philosophy, mind/body/spirit, and business titles form the cornerstone of our non-fiction list, we publish an exciting range of travel, current affairs, biography, and popular science books as well. Our renewed focus on popular fiction is evident in our new titles by a host of fresh young talent from India and abroad. Jaico's recently established translations division translates selected English content into nine regional languages.

Jaico distributes its own titles. With its headquarters in Mumbai, Jaico has branches in Ahmedabad, Bangalore, Chennai, Delhi, Hyderabad, and Kolkata.

SINCE 1946